BR STEAM MOTIVE POWER DEPOTS

SR

Paul Bolger

Nottingham

Booklaw Publications

Preface

Introduction

The purpose of this book is to assist the average enthusiast be he modeller, relic collector or historian, with his search for information on Motive Power Depots — the home of the steam locomotive.

Many devotees will recall the experience of touring such an establishment; the hiss of steam, the clank of engine movements and the sight of smoke suspended from the ceilings above the many varieties of engine in different stages of repair.

The sight of a fully serviced locomotive simmering outside the Depot on a crisp bright morning is a memory I shall never forget. I hope that the following pages aid the reminiscences of those fortunate enough to have lived during the steam age.

This book is dedicated to my wife Anne for her patient acceptance of my time spent compiling these books.

Paul Bolger

For reasons of parity with the previous volumes — *BR Steam Motive Power Depots: LMR, ER and ScR* (all Ian Allan) — the depots covered by this work have been restricted to those which possessed a code, as these were the most visited and of greater importance to the railway network.

In all, 38 depots are outlined and because of the lesser number of sheds by comparison with previous volumes four views per shed have been included, with a few exceptions. For continuity of the text the codes used as headings are c1950.

Acknowledgements

This book has been made possible with the invaluable help of the following people and organisations: Mr R. J. Collins and Mr W. F. C. Phillips of Bristol Divisional Civil Engineers Dept. British Rail; Mr G. M. Kitchenside of Locomotive & General Railway Photographs; Miss S. Percy of the Ordnance Survey; Mr C. Turner of Photomatic; Dr P. E. Cattermole of the Somerset & Dorset Railway Trust; Mr D. Wood of the Worcester Locomotive Society

In addition, special thanks are extended to the following: B. J. Ashworth; J. C. Beckett; J. Bentley; R. Blencowe; H. D. Bowtell; D. Carville; H. C. Casserley; G. S. Cocks; F. Dean; A. G. Ellis; K. Fairey; B. K. B. Green; P. H. Groom; B. Hilton; M. S. Houlgrave; B. H. Jackson; P. J. Kelly; F. Lyon; D. Milton; B. Morrison; N. D. Mundy; T. Nicholls; J. Oatway; J. A. Peden; I. Peters; W. Potter; N. E. Preedy; G. Reeve; D. Rendell; R. C. Riley; G. F. Roose; D. T. Rowe; R. E. Ruffell; T. V. Runnacles; J. Scrace; G. W. Sharpe, J. L. Smith, J. L. Stevenson; W. T. Stubbs; T. Wright.

In the course of preparation the following publications were of major importance as reference and consultative material: *The Railway Observer* (Volumes 18 to 38); *The Railway Magazine* (Volumes 94 to 114); *Railway World* (Volumes 19 to 29); *Trains Illustrated* & *Modern Railways* (Volumes 3 to 21).

First published 1983

*This edition published by
Book Law Publications 2009*

*Printed and Bound by
The Amadeus Press, Cleckheaton, BD19 4TQ.*

Notes about Contents

The ex-Somerset & Dorset Joint Railway establishments at Bath, Templecombe and Highbridge have been included within as 71G, 71H, and 71J respectively. They became Southern Region depots in 1950 and spent a good deal of their remaining lifetimes as part of the region.

The depots at Weymouth and Yeovil Pen Mill will be included in the Western Region volume as 82F and 82E respectively, as their origins were GWR and they did not become part of the Southern Region until 1958.

Pre-Grouping Origins

Although, primarily not relevant to the period covered, an indication of the vintage of the shed is given by the inclusion of the company of ownership prior to 1923. This is not necessarily the company which commissioned the building, as many smaller installations were absorbed into the larger companies by the takeover or amalgamation of district railways.

Gazetteer References

These numbers refer to the page and square within the Ian Allan *Pre-Grouping Atlas* which pinpoint the subject's national location.

Closing Dates

The dates given indicate the closure of the depot to steam engines only. However, in some cases the date would have been the same for diesels where the building closed completely, either as a result of its dilapidated condition or the effects of the 'Beeching' cuts.

Shed-Codes

The Southern Region was not issued with shed-codes at the outset of nationalisation in 1948 owing to BR's indecision over districts. In 1950 it was allocated ex-LMS type codes commencing with 70A. A full list of all codes is given on page 98.

Allocations

Where the depot's lifetime allows, three separate allocations, of steam locomotives only, are listed from the years 1950, 1959 and 1965. These lists are accurate to August 1950, May 1959 and May 1965.

Very few sets of allocations are in absolute numerical order as preference has been given to listing the locos in classification groups to keep this book on a par with previous volumes. The Southern Region loco-numbering system differed from other areas in that it did not allocate an exclusive batch of numbers for every class of engine. Many different classes were affected by this random method and the resulting lists are as consecutive as this format will allow.

Plans

All the plans have been based upon the Ordnance Survey County and National Grid series maps from various years and reproduction is by permission of the Controller of Her Majesty's Stationery Office, Crown Copyright Reserved.

Photographs

All except 18 of the 164 illustrations have been restricted to the period 1948/67. The majority of the views are hitherto unpublished and represent many years of search.

70A NINE ELMS

Pre-Grouping Origin: LSWR
Gazetteer Ref: 40 D5
Closed: 1967
Shed Code: 70A (1950-1967)
Allocations: 1950

Class M7 0-4-4T

30038	30132	30248	30322
30123	30241	30249	30667
30130	30244	30319	30676

Class T9   4-4-0
30119   30718

Class G6 0-6-0T
30160   30259   30353

Class L11 4-4-0
30163   30165   30405   30406

Class 02 0-4-4T
30221

Class H15 4-6-0

30332	30335	30484	30487
30333	30476	30485	30488
30334	30482	30486	30490

Class 700 0-6-0
30339   30692   30694   30699   30701

Class K10 4-4-0
30390

Class T14 4-6-0
30446   30461

'King Arthur' 4-6-0
30742 *Camelot*
30745 *Tintagel*
30747 *Elaine*
30755 *The Red Knight*
30765 *Sir Gareth*
30773 *Sir Lavaine*
30780 *Sir Persant*
30782 *Sir Brian*
30787 *Sir Menadeuke*
30791 *Sir Uwaine*
30792 *Sir Hervis de Revel*

'Lord Nelson' 4-6-0
30858 *Lord Duncan*
30859 *Lord Hood*
30860 *Lord Hawke*

Class Z 0-8-0T
30955

Class H 0-4-4T
31551   31552   31553   31554

Class U 2-6-0
31613   31619   31625   31637   31807

Classes E1 0-6-0T* and E4 0-6-2T
32138*   32468   32493   32500

'Battle of Britain' 4-6-2
34049 *Anti-Aircraft Command*
34050 *Royal Observer Corps*
34051 *Winston Churchill*
34052 *Lord Dowding*
34053 *Sir Keith Park*
34054 *Lord Beaverbrook*
34055 *Fighter Pilot*
34056 *Croydon*
34057 *Biggin Hill*
34058 *Sir Frederick Pile*
34059 *Sir Archibald Sinclair*
34060 *25 Squadron*
34061 *73 Squadron*
34062 *17 Squadron*
34063 *229 Squadron*
34064 *Fighter Command*
34065 *Hurricane*

Looking north-west to Nine Elms shed in 1959 with Class E4 0-6-2T No 32498 (70A) nearest the camera. The 'Old' and 'New' sheds are left and right respectively.   N. E. Preedy

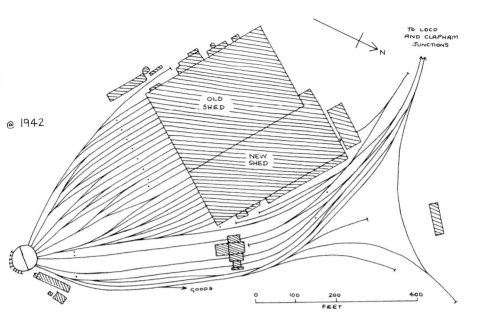

@ 1942

OLD SHED

NEW SHED

TO LOCO AND CLAPHAM JUNCTIONS

N

GOODS

| 0 | 100 | 200 | 400 |

FEET

'Merchant Navy' 4-6-2
35005 *Canadian Pacific*
35010 *Blue Star*
35011 *General Steam Navigation*
35012 *United States Line*
35013 *Blue Funnel*
35014 *Nederland Line*
35015 *Rotterdam Lloyd*
35016 *Elders Fyffes*
35017 *Belgian Marine*
35018 *British India Line*
35019 *French Line CGT*
35020 *Bibby Line*

Total 99

Allocations: 1959

Class 57xx 0-6-0PT
4634   4686   4698
4672   4692   9770

Class M7 0-4-4T
30123   30241   30248   30319   30321
30133   30245   30249   30320

Class T9 4-4-0
30338   30718   30719

'King Arthur' 4-6-0
30457 *Sir Bedivere*
30763 *Sir Bors de Ganis*
30774 *Sir Gaheris*
30778 *Sir Pelleas*
30779 *Sir Colgrevance*

Class H15 4-6-0
30482   30486   30491   30522   30524
30484   30489   30521   30523

Class 700 0-6-0
30694   30699   30701

'Schools' 4-4-0
30902 *Wellington*
30903 *Charterhouse*
30906 *Sherborne*
30907 *Dulwich*

Class U 2-6-0
31617   31621   31624   31634   31796

Class E4 0-6-2T
32487   32497   32498   32500   32563

Class Q1 0-6-0
33015   33017   33038

'West Country' 4-6-2
34006 *Bude*
34007 *Wadebridge*
34009 *Lyme Regis*
34010 *Sidmouth*
34018 *Axminster*
34020 *Seaton*
34029 *Lundy*
34031 *Torrington*
34047 *Callington*
34093 *Saunton*
34094 *Mortehoe*
34095 *Brentor*

'Battle of Britain' 4-6-2
34064 *Fighter Command*
34065 *Hurricane*
34090 *Sir Eustace Missenden,*
          Southern Railway

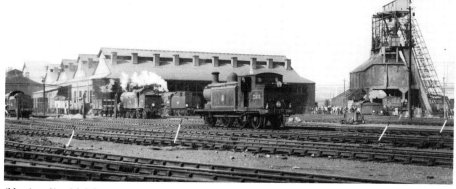

'Merchant Navy' 4-6-2
35005 *Canadian Pacific*
35012 *United States Lines*
35014 *Nederland Line*
35016 *Elders Fyffes*
35017 *Belgian Marine*
35018 *British India Line*
35019 *French Line CGT*
35020 *Bibby Line*
35029 *Ellerman Lines*
35030 *Elder Dempster Lines*

Class 5 4-6-0
73087
73088
73089 *Maid of Astolat*

73110	73112	73114	73116	73118
73111	73113	73115	73117	73119
				Total 90

An easterly view of Nine Elms coaler in 1967 together with 'Merchant Navy' 4-6-2 No 35013 Blue Funnel *(70F).* K. Fairey

Nine Elms 'New' Shed and coaling plant in 1959. W. Potter

Allocations: 1965

'West Country' 4-6-2
34001 *Exeter*
34002 *Salisbury*
34021 *Dartmoor*
34038 *Lynton*

Class 5MT 4-6-0
| 73016 | 73065 |
73081 *Excalibur*
73082 *Camelot*
73084 *Tintagel*
73085 *Melisande*
73086 *The Green Knight*
73088 *Joyous Gard*
73112 *Morgan le Fay*

Class 4MT 4-6-0
| 75069 | 75074 | 75077 |
| 75070 | 75076 | 75078 |

The last day of steam traction on the Southern Region, 9 July 1967 and a sorry looking Nine Elms as viewed from the turntable. A handful of locos occupy the roofless 'Old' shed and groups of spotters pay their last respects. G. S. Cocks

Class 4MT 2-6-4T

80069	80133	80143
80095	80137	80154

Class 3MT 2-6-2T

82005	82019	82022	82026	82029
82006	82020	82023	82027	82033
82018	82021	82024	82028	

Total 39

Nine Elms was among the last seven sheds on the Southern Region which closed to steam in July 1967. The remaining locos went for scrap.

70B FELTHAM

Pre-Grouping Origin: LSWR
Gazetteer Ref: 5 B2
Closed: 1967
Shed Code: 70B (1950-1967)
Allocations: 1950

Class M7 0-4-4T

30043	30254

Class L11 4-4-0

30164	30174	30414	30438

Class 700 0-6-0

30309	30352	30688	30696	30698
30346	30687	30689	30697	

Class T9 4-4-0

30311	30732

Class H15 4-6-0

30330	30331

Class K10 4-4-0

30384

Class G16 4-8-0T

30492	30493	30494	30495

Class S15 4-6-0

30496	30502	30508	30514	30837
30497	30503	30509	30515	30838
30498	30504	30510	30833	30839
30499	30505	30511	30834	30840
30500	30506	30512	30835	
30501	30507	30513	30836	

Class H16 4-6-2T

30516	30517	30518	30519	30520

Class 0395 0-6-0

30567	30570	30573
30569	30572	30579

'King Arthur' 4-6-0
30738 *King Pellinore*

Class U 2-6-0
31624

Class Q1 0-6-0

33006	33008	33010	33012
33007	33009	33011	33013

Class WD 2-8-0

90257	90562	90570	90604

Total 77

Allocations: 1959

Class M7 0-4-4T

30032	30043

Class 02 0-4-4T

30177	30179

Class 700 0-6-0

30339	30352	30687	30696
30346	30355	30689	

Class G16 4-8-0T

30493	30494	30495

The western end of Feltham depot in 1959 with (left to right), 'S15' 4-6-0 No 30832 (72B), 'U1' 2-6-0 No 31892 (70B), 'H16' 4-6-2T No 30516 (70B) and 'S15' 4-6-0 No 30498 (70B).   N. E. Preedy

Class S15 4-6-0

30496	30501	30506	30511	30833
30497	30502	30507	30512	30834
30498	30503	30508	30513	30838
30499	30504	30509	30514	30839
30500	30505	30510	30515	30840

Class H16 4-6-2T

30516	30517	30518	30519	30520

Class 0395
30567

Class T9 4-4-0
30732

Class C2 0-6-0

32437	32438

Class Q1 0-6-0

33006	33009	33012	33018
33007	33010	33013	33026
33008	33011	33016	33027

Total 60

Allocations: 1965

Class S15 4-6-0

30824	30837	30839
30833	30838	30842

Class 4MT 2-6-0

76053	76055	76066

Total 9

Feltham closed at the end of steam traction on the Southern Region in July 1967 and its few remaining locos went for scrap.

Although the shed was not fully operational until early Southern Railway days it has been afforded LSWR origin because the latter company commenced building prior to the 1923 Grouping.

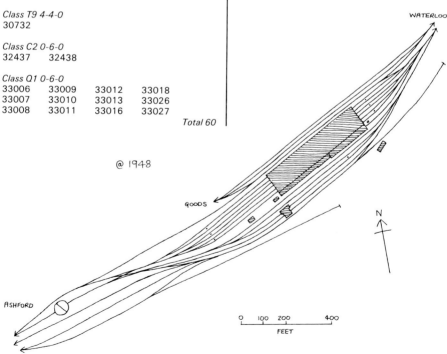

@ 1948

WATERLOO

GOODS

ASHFORD

N

| 0 | 100 | 200 | 400 |
FEET

Looking east to Feltham shed and coaler in Southern Railway days. Ian Allan Library

Another view of Feltham in SR days taken from a different angle. Lens of Sutton

The eastern end of Feltham showing the single ended repair bay alongside the running shed. Lens of Sutton

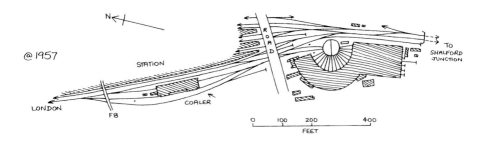

@1957

N←

STATION

LONDON

FB

COALER

ROAD

TO SHALFORD JUNCTION

0   100   200   400
FEET

70C   GUILDFORD

Pre-Grouping Origin: LSWR
Gazetteer Ref: 5 C1
Closed: 1967
Shed-Code: 70C (1950 to 1967)
Allocations: 1950

Class M7 0-4-4T

30021	30056	30110	30328
30022	30060	30246	30481
30026	30108	30324	

Class L11 4-4-0

30158	30436

Class G6 0-6-0T

30268	30270	30349

Class T9 4-4-0

30281	30312	30336	30710

Class 700 0-6-0

30308	30325	30326	30327

Class L12 4-4-0

30416	30420	30425	30428

Class 0458 0-4-0ST
30458 *Ironside*

Class 0395 0-6-0

30565	30574	30576	30578	30580
30568	30575			

Class U 2-6-0

31620	31628	31635	31801
31621	31629	31798	31802
31627	31630	31800	31804

Class E4 0-6-2T
32490

The last day of steam traction on the Southern Region, 9 July 1967 this time at Guildford. Shed pilot No 30072 shunts a van from the turntable as 'West Country' 4-6-2 No 34018 Axminster (minus nameplates) (70A) prepares to leave with the shed stores.   Ian Allan Library

Class Q1 0-6-0

33001	33003	33005	33015
33002	33004	33014	33016

Total 57

Allocations: 1959

Class M7 0-4-4T

30026	30124	30132	30246

Class B4 0-4-0T

30089

Class G6 0-6-0T

30238	30277	30349

Class 700 0-6-0

30308	30326	30693	30698
30325	30350	30697	30700

Looking north to the Guildford coaling plant in 1964 with Class 5MT 4-6-0 No 73168 (70B) facing.
W. Potter

Class T9 4-4-0

30724

Class U 2-6-0

31612	31627	31635	31798
31616	31628	31636	31799
31622	31630	31637	31800
31625	31631	31797	31807

A southerly view of Guildford shed in 1962 from the nearby road overbridge. Class B4 0-4-0T No 30089 acting as shed pilot can be seen reversing on to the over-girder turntable.   P. H. Groom

Guildford by night in 1956 showing the newly fitted lighting. Locos left to right are Nos 30338 (70A), 33018 (70B), 31611 (70D), 31622 (70C), 30325 (70C), 33004 (70C). Ian Allan Library

Guildford shed closed at the end of steam traction on the Southern Region in July 1967. The surviving engines were thus withdrawn from service.

As the allocation lists verify, Guildford's shed pilot was updated over the years: Nos 30458 *Ironside* (1950), 30089 (1959) and 30072 (1965). Their respective withdrawal dates were June 1954, March 1963 and July 1967.

Class C 0-6-0

31722	31723

Class E4 0-6-2T

32505	32506

Class Q1 0-6-0

33001	33003	33005	33022
33002	33004	33019	33025

Total 45

Allocations: 1965

Class USA 0-6-0T

30072

Class N 2-6-0

31401	31411	31816	31858	31873
31408	31811	31842	31866	

Class U 2-6-0

31619	31639	31791	31803
31627	31790	31800	31809

Class Q1 0-6-0

33006	33018	33026
33009	33020	33027

Class 2 MT 2-6-2T

41287	41294	41299	41301

Total 28

70D   BASINGSTOKE

Pre-Grouping Origin: LSWR
Gazetteer Ref: 4 B2
Closed: 1967
Shed-Code: 70D (1950 to 1963)
Allocations: 1950

Class G6 0-6-0T

30258	30266

Class T9 4-4-0

30302	30712

Class 700 0-6-0

30368	30693

Class L12 4-4-0

30418

'King Arthur' 4-6-0

30451 *Sir Lamorak*
30456 *Sir Galahad*

Basingstoke shed in July 1967, three days before
closure. An unidentified BR Standard is prepared for
the road beside a lifeless diesel.   J. L. Stevenson

Basingstoke from the west in 1956 with the station
visible beyond the right hand side. 'King Arthur' class
No 30763 Sir Bors de Ganis (70D) simmers on the
left whilst facing are Class H15 4-6-0 No 30475
(71A) and '700' 0-6-0 No 30368 (70D).   W. Potter

This 1962 view of Basingstoke clearly spells out the
threat of oncoming diesels. Class 4 4-6-0 No 75078
(70D) is on the left.   W. Potter

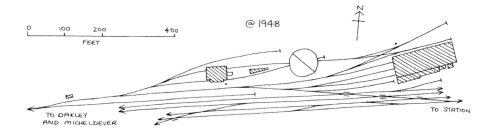

@ 1948

```
O        100    200        400
         FEET
```

TO OAKLEY
AND MICHELDEVER

TO STATION

Class U 2-6-0
31633

Class B4X 4-4-0
32045   32052   32067

Class E1 0-6-0T
32160

'Remembrance' 4-6-0
32327 Trevithick
32328 Hackworth
32329 Stephenson
32330 Cudworth
32331 Beattie
32332 Stroudley
32333 Remembrance

Total 21

Allocations: 1959

Class G6 0-6-0T
30258

Class 700 0-6-0
30368

'King Arthur' 4-6-0
30456 Sir Galahad
30765 Sir Gareth
30794 Sir Ector de Maris

'Schools' 4-4-0
30904 Lancing
30905 Tonbridge
30923 Bradfield

Class U 2-6-0
31611   31806

Class 4 4-6-0
75076   75077   75078   75079

Total 14

Basingstoke shed lost its coded status in March 1963 when its engines moved to Nine Elms 70A, Guildford 70C and Eastleigh 71A. The depot remained open as a signing-on point until the end of steam traction on the Southern Region.

The 1950 allocation shows that all the 'Remembrance' class 4-6-0s (sometimes referred to as 'N15X') were shedded here. The last one, No 32331, *Beattie*, was withdrawn from Basingstoke in July 1957.

A Class V2 2-6-2 at Basingstoke in 1966, namely No 60919 from 62B Dundee Tay Bridge! This engine was booked to pull the LCGB special from Waterloo to Salisbury and Weymouth on 3 July but became defective and No 34002 had to be substituted.
B. H. Jackson

70E   READING

Pre-Grouping Origin: SECR
Gazetteer Ref: 4 A2
Closed: 1965
Shed–Code: 70E (1950 to 1959)
Allocations: 1950

Class D 4-4-0
31057   31075   31740   31744   31750

Class B1 4-4-0
31443

Class E 4-4-0
31515

Class T 0-6-0T
31602   31604

Class U 2-6-0
31610   31614   31794   31797
31611   31615   31796   31799

Total 17

The gradual running down of Reading (South) began in May 1954 when most of its allocation transferred to Redhill (75B) and Guildford (70C). The last two engines went to store in December 1956 and the shed became a sub of Basingstoke (70D) in 1959. Guildford (70C) became its parent depot in 1960 and complete closure was in January 1965.

The eastern end of Reading in 1961 with locos (left to right) 'Schools' 4-4-0 No 30909 St Paul's *(70C) and 'U' 2-6-0 No 31617 (70A). The former engine was withdrawn in February 1962 and cut up shortly afterwards (see Ashford Works view — 74A).*
N. D. Mundy

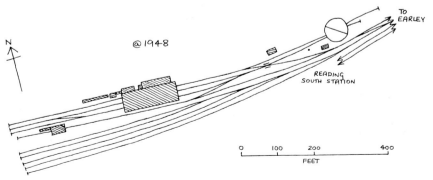

@ 1948

TO EARLEY

READING SOUTH STATION

0   100   200   400
FEET

N

15

Reading South in 1962 with Class N 2-6-0
No 31817 (75B) and 'S15' 4-6-0 No 30845 (72A)
at rest outside.   N. E. Preedy

Class 700 0-6-0 No 30346 (70B) stands outside
Reading in 1959.   R. C. Riley

Ugly but effective. An austere 'Q1' class 0-6-0,
namely No 33019 (70C) on shed at Reading in
1963.   K. Fairey

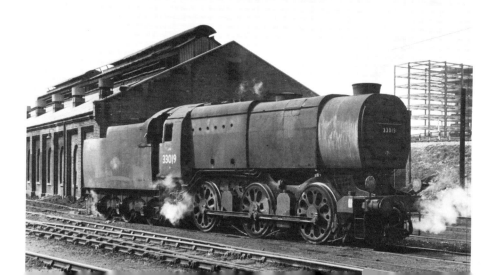

71A EASTLEIGH

Pre-Grouping Origin: LSWR
Gazetteer Ref: 4 D3
Closed: 1967
Shed-Codes: 71A (1950 to 1963)
70D (1963 to 1967)
Allocations: 1950 (71A)

Class M7 0-4-4T

30029	30033	30109	30242	30479
30031	30048	30125	30357	30673
30032	30053	30128	30378	30674

Class B4 0-4-0T
30082
30083
30089 *Trouville*

Class T9 4-4-0

30121	30287	30313	30711	30722
30282	30300	30705	30713	30729
30286	30304	30708	30721	

Class L11 4-4-0

30148	30156	30171	30411	30442
30154	30157	30173	30413	
30155	30159	30175	30437	

Class O2 0-4-4T

30213	30225	30233

Class 700 0-6-0

30306	30316	30350	30700

Class T1 0-4-4T
30367

Class S11 4-4-0
30401

Class L12 4-4-0

30422	30429	30431	30433
30423	30430	30432	30434

Class D15 4-4-0

30463	30465	30467	30469	30471
30464	30466	30468	30470	30472

Class H15 4-6-0

30473	30477	30489	30522
30474	30478	30491	30523
30475	30483	30521	30524

Class Q 0-6-0

30530	30532	30536	30543
30531	30535	30542	30544

Class 0395 0-6-0

30566	30571

Class C14 0-4-0T

30588	30589

'King Arthur' 4-6-0
30749 *Iseult*
30752 *Linette*
30772 *Sir Percivale*
30777 *Sir Lamiel*
30779 *Sir Colgrevance*
30783 *Sir Gillemere*
30784 *Sir Nerovens*
30785 *Sir Mador de la Porte*
30788 *Sir Urre of the Mount*
30789 *Sir Guy*
30790 *Sir Villiars*

'Lord Nelson' 4-6-0
30850 *Lord Nelson*
30851 *Sir Francis Drake*
30852 *Sir Walter Raleigh*
30853 *Sir Richard Grenville*
30854 *Howard of Effingham*
30855 *Robert Blake*
30856 *Lord St Vincent*
30857 *Lord Howe*

The southern end of Eastleigh shed in 1964 with 'Merchant Navy' Class 4-6-2 No 35026 Lamport & Holt Line *(83D) nearest the camera.* W. Potter

17

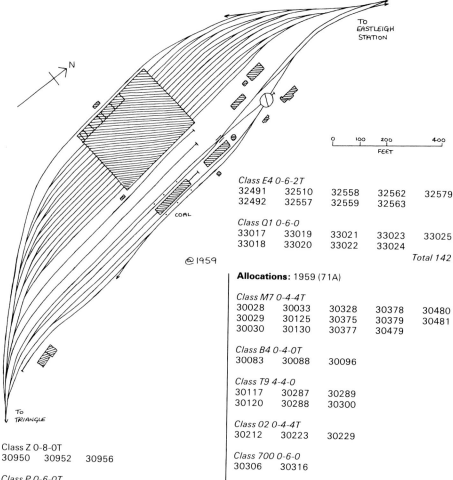

N

To
EASTLEIGH
STATION

@ 1959

COAL

To
TRIANGLE

0	100	200	400

FEET

Class E4 0-6-2T

32491	32510	32558	32562	32579
32492	32557	32559	32563	

Class Q1 0-6-0

33017	33019	33021	33023	33025
33018	33020	33022	33024	

Total 142

Allocations: 1959 (71A)

Class M7 0-4-4T

30028	30033	30328	30378	30480
30029	30125	30375	30379	30481
30030	30130	30377	30479	

Class B4 0-4-0T

30083	30088	30096

Class T9 4-4-0

30117	30287	30289
30120	30288	30300

Class 02 0-4-4T

30212	30223	30229

Class 700 0-6-0

30306	30316

Class H15 4-6-0

30473	30474	30475	30476	30477

Looking across Eastleigh shed yard in 1962 with a pair of 'A1X' class 0-6-0Ts on the left. There were five of these diminutive veterans allocated to the shed in this year. J. L. Stevenson

Class Z 0-8-0T
30950   30952   30956

Class P 0-6-0T
31325

Class N 2-6-0
31828   31866   31867

Class E1 0-6-0T
32133   32147

Class Q 0-6-0

30530	30532	30536	30543
30531	30535	30542	

'King Arthur' 4-6-0
30770 *Sir Prianius*
30773 *Sir Lavaine*
30784 *Sir Nerovens*
30785 *Sir Mador de la Porte*
30786 *Sir Lionel*
30788 *Sir Urre of the Mount*
30789 *Sir Guy*
30790 *Sir Villiars*
30791 *Sir Uwaine*

'Lord Nelson' 4-6-0
30850 *Lord Nelson*
30851 *Sir Francis Drake*
30852 *Sir Walter Raleigh*
30853 *Sir Richard Grenville*
30854 *Howard of Effingham*
30855 *Robert Blake*
30856 *Lord St Vincent*
30857 *Lord Howe*
30858 *Lord Duncan*
30859 *Lord Hood*
30861 *Lord Anson*
30862 *Lord Collingwood*
30863 *Lord Rodney*

Class U 2-6-0

31618	31629	31793	31801	31808
31619	31639	31794	31802	
31620	31792	31795	31803	

Class E4 0-6-2T

32491	32510	32556	32559	32579

Class Q1 0-6-0

33020	33021	33023

Class 2 2-6-2T

41293	41305

Class 4 2-6-0

76010	76015	76025	76063	76068
76011	76016	76026	76064	76069
76012	76017	76027	76065	
76013	76018	76028	76066	
76014	76019	76029	76067	

Class 3 2-6-2T

82012	82014	82015	82016

Total 111

As the end of steam traction approaches, Class 2MT 2-6-2T No 41319 (70D) and 'West Country' 4-6-2 No 34018 Axminster (70A) stands alongside the Eastleigh coaling plant in February 1967.   W. Potter

Allocations: 1965 (70D)

Class USA 0-6-0T

30064	30067	30069	30071	30073

'West Country' 4-6-2
34004 *Yeovil*
34008 *Padstow*
34009 *Lyme Regis*
34017 *Ilfracombe*
34018 *Axminster*
34019 *Bideford*
34023 *Blackmore Vale*
34025 *Whimple*
34033 *Chard*
34034 *Honiton*
34036 *Westward Ho*
34037 *Clovelly*
34039 *Boscastle*
34041 *Wilton*
34042 *Dorchester*
34093 *Saunton*
34095 *Brentor*
34097 *Holsworthy*
34098 *Templecombe*
34101 *Hartland*
34102 *Lapford*
34103 *Calstock*
34104 *Bere Alston*

'Battle of Britain' 4-6-2
34050 *Royal Observer Corps*
34060 *25 Squadron*
34064 *Fighter Command*
34071 *601 Squadron*
34076 *41 Squadron*
34077 *603 Squadron*
34079 *141 Squadron*
34082 *615 Squadron*
34084 *253 Squadron*
34086 *219 Squadron*
34087 *145 Squadron*
34088 *213 Squadron*
34090 *Sir Eustace Missenden,
Southern Railway*

'Remembrance' class 4-6-0 No 32328 Hackworth (70D) and 'Lord Nelson' 4-6-0 No 30859 Lord Hood (70A) stand in line at Eastleigh in 1953. The former class were entirely allocated to Basingstoke and the last one (No 32331 Beattie) was withdrawn in 1957. K. Fairey

Class 2MT 2-6-2T
41313   41319   41325

Class 5MT 4-6-0
73022   73029   73037   73041   73043
73087 *Linette*
73089 *Maid of Astolat*
73092   73093
73110 *The Red Knight*
73111 *King Uther*
73113 *Lyonnesse*
73114 *Etarre*
73115 *King Pellinore*
73117 *Vivien*
73118 *King Leodegrance*
73119 *Elaine*
73155   73168   73169   73170   73171

Class 4MT 4-6-0
75065   75066   75068   75075   75079

Class 4MT 2-6-0
76006   76012   76031   76060   76064
76009   76016   76033   76061   76065
76010   76018   76058   76062   76068
76011   76019   76059   76063   76069

Class 4MT 2-6-4T
80012   80065   80082   80132
80015   80066   80083   80139
80016   80070   80102   80150

Total 103

Eastleigh survived until the end of steam on the Southern Region in July 1967 and its remaining engines went for scrap.

As the allocations suggest, Eastleigh was one of the most important depots on the Southern Region as it was responsible for Southampton's dock traffic movements.

71B   BOURNEMOUTH

Pre-Grouping Origin: LSWR
Gazetteer Ref: 3 F5
Closed: 1967
Shed-Codes: 71B (1950-1963)
70F (1963-1967)
Allocations: 1950 (71B)

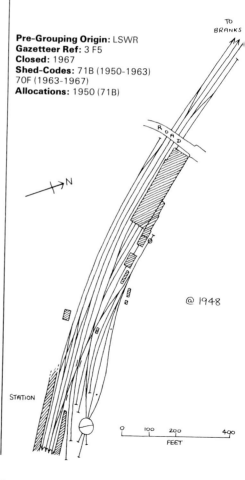

Bournemouth shed in 1965. 'West Country' class 4-6-2 No 34034 Honiton *(70D) is nearest the camera.* D. Wood

Class M7 0-4-4T

30028	30052	30104	30112	30318
30040	30057	30106	30131	30379
30051	30059	30111	30251	

Class B4 0-4-0T
30086 *Havre*
30087
30093 *St Malo*

Class 02 0-4-4T
30204   30212

Class G6 0-6-0T
30260

Class S11 4-4-0
30398   30403   30404

This 1966 view of Bournemouth shows two Class 5MT 4-6-0s Nos 73088 Joyous Gard *(minus nameplates) and 73093 (both 70C) with 'West Country' 4-6-2 No 34037* Clovelly *(70A) on the right.* J. L. Stevenson

Class Q 0-6-0
30548   30549

Class 700 0-6-0
30695

Class T9 4-4-0
30728

'King Arthur' 4-6-0
30736 *Excalibur*
30737 *King Uther*
30740 *Merlin*
30741 *Joyous Gard*
30743 *Lyonnesse*
30746 *Pendragon*
30750 *Morgan le Fay*
30751 *Etarre*
30754 *The Green Knight*

'Lord Nelson' 4-6-0
30861 *Lord Anson*
30862 *Lord Collingwood*
30863 *Lord Rodney*
30864 *Sir Martin Frobisher*
30865 *Sir John Hawkins*

Class U 2-6-0
31622   31632   31795

'West Country' 4-6-2
34093 *Saunton*
34094 *Mortehoe*
34095 *Brentor*
34105 *Swanage*
34106 *Lydford*
34107 *Blandford Forum*
34108 *Wincanton*

'Battle of Britain' 4-6-2
34109 *Sir Trafford Leigh-Mallory*

Total 52

Allocations: 1959 (71B)

Class M7 0-4-4T

30040	30060	30107	30127
30057	30104	30108	30128
30058	30105	30111	30318
30059	30106	30112	30324

Class B4 0-4-0T
30093   30102

Class G6 0-6-0T
30274

Class T9 4-4-0
30310   30706   30707

Looking east to Bournemouth shed yard in 1966.
R. E. Ruffell

Class Q 0-6-0
30539   30541   30548

Class 700 0-6-0
30690   30695

'King Arthur' 4-6-0
30764 *Sir Gawain*
30771 *Sir Sagramore*
30772 *Sir Percivale*
30780 *Sir Persant*
30781 *Sir Aglovale*
30782 *Sir Brian*
30783 *Sir Gillemere*

'Lord Nelson' 4-6-0
30860 *Lord Hawke*
30864 *Sir Martin Frobisher*
30865 *Sir John Hawkins*

Bournemouth shed in 1962 as viewed from the
direction of the station.   B. H. Jackson

Class U 2-6-0
31614   31615   31632

'West Country' 4-6-2
34028 Eddystone
34039 Boscastle
34040 Crewkerne
34041 Wilton
34042 Dorchester
34043 Combe Martin
34044 Woolacombe
34045 Ottery St Mary
34046 Braunton
34048 Crediton
34102 Lapford
34105 Swanage
34107 Blandford Forum

'Merchant Navy' 4-6-2
35002 Union Castle
35010 Blue Star
35021 New Zealand Line
35022 Holland-America Line
35024 East Asiatic Company
35025 Brocklebank Line
35027 Port Line
                                Total 60

Allocations: 1965 (70F)

'West Country' 4-6-2
34024 Tamar Valley
34040 Crewkerne
34044 Woolacombe
34046 Braunton
34047 Callington

'Battle of Britain' 4-6-2
34053 Sir Keith Park
34085 501 Squadron

'Merchant Navy' 4-6-2
35003 Royal Mail
35004 Cunard White Star
35008 Orient Line
35010 Blue Star
35011 General Steam Navigation
35013 Blue Funnel
35021 New Zealand Line
35023 Holland-Afrika Line
35027 Port Line

Class 2MT 2-6-2T
41224   41275   41312   41316
41230   41295   41314   41320

Class 4MT 2-6-0
76013   76015   76026   76056
76014   76025   76027   76057

Class 4MT 2-6-4T
80013   80096   80138   80147
80081   80134   80146
                                Total 39

Bournemouth shed closed to steam in July 1967 and its remaining engines went for scrap.

71C DORCHESTER

Pre-Grouping Origin: LSWR
Gazetteer Ref: 3 F3
Closed: 1957
Shed-Code: 71C (1950 to 1955)
Allocations: 1950

Class T9 4-4-0
30116   30284   30307   30338

Class G6 0-6-0T
30162

Class 02 0-4-4T
30177   30197   30229
30179   30223   30231

Class S11 4-4-0
30399

Class L12 4-4-0
30415   30424
                                Total 14

Dorchester shed declined in importance after nationalisation and eventually lost its code in March 1955 and became a sub-shed to Bournemouth 71B. The depot closed completely in July 1957 and demolition followed soon after.

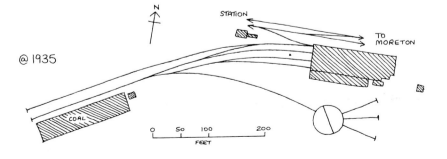

Looking east to Dorchester shed in 1950.
LGRP courtesy of David & Charles Ltd

A Southern Railway's view of Dorchester in 1929
clearly showing the separate stages of construction.
Whilst the left hand portion is the original, both
structures were of mid-19th century vintage as the
identical window patterns illustrated here would
confirm.   H. C. Casserley

Dorchester in 1939 as viewed from the station.
K. O. B. Nichols

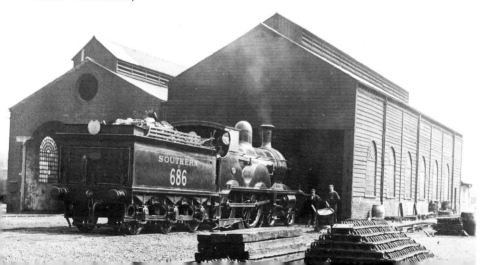

71D   FRATTON

Pre-Grouping Origin: LSWR/LBSCR Joint
Gazetteer Ref: 4 E2
Closed: 1959
Shed-Codes: 71D (1950 to 1954)
70F (1954 to 1959)
Allocations: 1950 (71D)

Class T1 0-4-4T
30020

Class M7 0-4-4T
30045   30050   30054   30480

Class T9 4-4-0

30113	30118	30285	30310	30731
30114	30120	30303	30314	30733
30115	30280	30305	30726	

Class L11 4-4-0
30170   30172   30441

Class S11 4-4-0

30395	30396	30397	30400	30402

Class L12 4-4-0

30417	30419	30426	30427

Class U 2-6-0
31805   31809

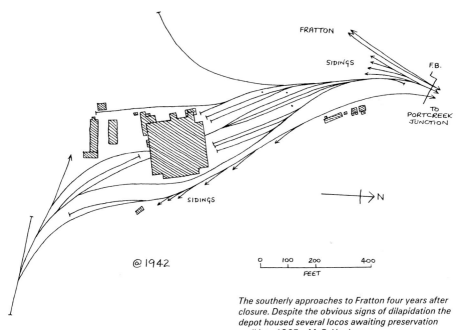

@ 1942

The southerly approaches to Fratton four years after
closure. Despite the obvious signs of dilapidation the
depot housed several locos awaiting preservation
well into 1965.   M. S. Houlgrave

Class N 2-6-0
31870

Class E1 0-6-0T
32129   32691   32694

Class C3 0-6-0
32300   32301   32303   32306

Class K 2-6-0
32338   32340

Fratton shed yard and north entrance in 1959 with Class M7 0-4-4T No 30039 and 'U' 2-6-0 No 31805 (both 70F) left and centre respectively.   P. J. Kelley

Inside Fratton roundhouse in 1963 showing two of the locos stored awaiting preservation. Left is 'Lord Nelson' Class 4-6-0 No 30850 Lord Nelson *and right 'King Aurthur' Class 4-6-0 No 30777* Sir Lamiel. *Note that the locos lengths have necessitated the uncoupling of the tenders.*   K. Fairey

Class E4 0-6-2T
32487

Class A1X 0-6-0T
32646   32655   32661   32662   32677
                                      Total 49

Allocations: 1959 (70F)

Class M7 0-4-4T
30039   30357

Class U 2-6-0
31638   31804   31805   31809

Class K 2-6-0
32337   32349

Class E4 0-6-2T
32479   32495   32509

Class C2 0-6-0
32548   32549   32550

Class A1X 0-6-0T
32640   32650   32677
32646   32661   32678

Class E1 0-6-0T
32694
                                      Total 21

Fratton shed closed in November 1959 and its remaining locos were dispersed to Eastleigh, Norwood Junction, Guildford, Three Bridges and Southampton Docks. The depot later housed some Southern Region locos awaiting preservation.

A 1964 view of Fratton interior showing some of the other stored locomotives. T. V. Runnacles

71E   NEWPORT IoW

Pre-Grouping Origin: IoW Central Railway
Gazetteer Ref: 4 F3
Closed: 1957
Shed-Codes: 71E (1950 to 1954)
70G (1954 to 1957)
Allocations: 1950 (71E)

Class E1 0-6-0T
W1 *Medina*
W2 *Yarmouth*
W3 *Ryde*
W4 *Wroxall*

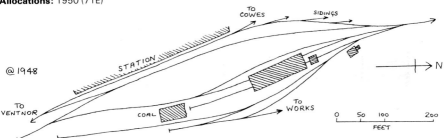

27

Class O2 0-4-4T
W26 *Whitwell*
W27 *Merstone*
W28 *Ashey*
W29 *Alverstone*
W30 *Shorwell*
W31 *Chale*
W32 *Bonchurch*
W33 *Bembridge*
W34 *Newport*
W35 *Freshwater*
W36 *Carisbrooke*

Total 15

Newport closed in November 1957 and the remaining engines transferred to Ryde 71F.

Newport (Isle of Wight) shed in 1939 from the south. The three locos in line are (left to right) Class E1 0-6-0T Nos 4 Wroxall, *2* Yarmouth *and Class O2 0-4-4T No 29* Alverstone.   N. E. Preedy

Newport in 1948 with Classes A1X 0-6-0T No 8 Freshwater *and E1 0-6-0T No 2* Yarmouth. *The last two 'Terriers' (Class A1X) on the island were Nos 8* Freshwater *and 13* Carisbrooke *and they returned to the mainland in May 1949.*
LGRP courtesy of David & Charles Ltd.

Newport shed in 1949 Real Photographs

Class E1 0-6-0T No 3 Ryde *outside Newport in 1956.* K. Fairey

71F   RYDE IoW

Pre-Grouping Origin: IoW Railway
Gazetteer Ref: 4 F3
Closed: 1967
Shed-Codes: 71F (1950 to 1954)
70H (1954 to 1967)
Allocations: 1950 (71F)

Class 02 0-4-4T
W14 *Fishbourne*
W15 *Cowes*
W16 *Ventnor*
W17 *Seaview*
W18 *Ningwood*
W19 *Osborne*
W20 *Shanklin*
W21 *Sandown*
W22 *Brading*
W23 *Totland*
W24 *Calbourne*
W25 *Godshill*

Total 12

Allocations: 1959 (70H)

Class E1 0-6-0T
W3 *Ryde*
W4 *Wroxall*

Class 02 0-4-4T
W14 *Fishbourne*
W16 *Ventnor*
W17 *Seaview*
W18 *Ningwood*
W20 *Shanklin*
W21 *Sandown*
W22 *Brading*
W24 *Calbourne*
W25 *Godshill*
W26 *Whitwell*
W27 *Merstone*
W28 *Ashey*
W29 *Alverstone*
W30 *Shorwell*
W31 *Chale*
W32 *Bonchurch*
W33 *Bembridge*
W35 *Freshwater*
W36 *Carisbrooke*

Total 21

Allocations: 1965 (70H)

Class 02 0-4-4T
W14 *Fishbourne*
W16 *Ventnor*
W17 *Seaview*
W18 *Ningwood*
W20 *Shanklin*
W21 *Sandown*
W22 *Brading*
W24 *Calbourne*
W26 *Whitwell*
W27 *Merstone*
W28 *Ashey*
W29 *Alverstone*
W30 *Shorwell*
W31 *Chale*
W33 *Bembridge*
W35 *Freshwater*

Total 16

Ryde closed in March 1967 when the Island was electrified and the last two locos (Nos W24 and W31) were withdrawn.

The abundance of motive power in the 1959 and 1965 listings over that of 1950 is misleading as in the latter year the Island's loco stud was shared with the Newport depot (see 71E).

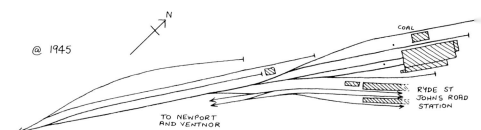

A line up of locos outside Ryde shed in 1959 with
'02' class 0-4-4T No 25 *Godshill* to the fore.
Photomatic

A pair of '02' class 0-4-4Ts at rest outside Ryde in 1964.   K. Fairey

Ryde works was situated on the eastern side of St Johns Road station and this 1956 view depicts '02' class 0-4-4T No 26 Whitwell *receiving attention under the sheer-legs.*   K. Fairey

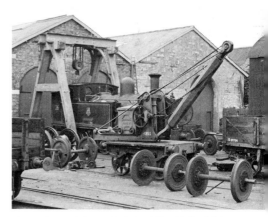

A superb posed view at Ryde in 1958 with five '02' class 0-4-4Ts on display. Left to right are Nos 30 Shorwell, 22 Brading, 27 Merstone, 29 Alverstone and 26 Whitwell. P. H. Groom

71G BATH (GREEN PARK)

Pre-Grouping Origin: SDJR/Mid Rly
Gazetteer Ref: 3 A3
Closed: 1966
Shed-Codes: 22C (1948 to 1950)
71G (1950 to 1958)
82F (1958 to 1966)
Allocations: 1950 (71G)

Class 2P 4-4-0
40505	40569	40696	40698
40568	40601	40697	40700

Class 2MT 2-6-2T
41240	41241	41242	41243

Class 4MT 2-6-0
43013	43017	43036

Class 4F 0-6-0
43875	44355	44535	44559
44096	44422	44557	44560
44235	44523	44558	44561

Class 5MT 4-6-0
44826	44830	44839	44945	45440

Sentinel 0-4-0T
47191

Class 3F 0-6-0T
47275	47465	47542
47316	47496	47557

Class OF 0-4-0T
51202

Class 7F 2-8-0
53800	53803	53806	53809
53801	53804	53807	53810
53802	53805	53808	

Total 51

Allocations: 1959 (82F)

Class 57xx 0-6-0PT
3742

Class 2P 4-4-0
40601	40696	40697	40698	40700

Class 2 2-6-2T
41241	41242	41243	41296	41304

Class 3F 0-6-0
43682

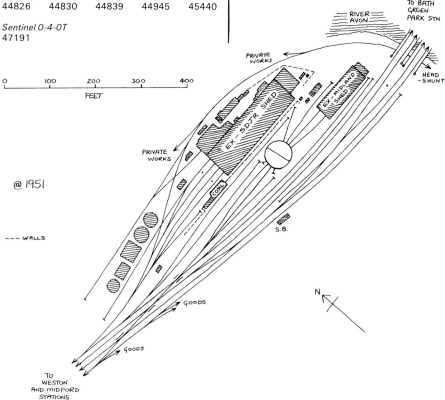

@ 1951

--- WALLS

*The ex-Midland building at Bath Green Park shed in
1960. Locos (left to right) are Class 3 2-6-2T
No 82041 (82F), Class 9F 2-10-0 No 92203 (82B),
Class 2 2-6-2T No 41242 (82F) and Class 4F 0-6-0
No 44146 (82F).* N. E. Preedy

Class 4F 0-6-0

44096	44422	44558	44560
44146	44523	44559	44561

Sentinel 0-4-0T

47190	47191

Class 3F 0-6-0T

47275	47316	47465	47496	47557

Class 7F 2-8-0

53800	53803	53806	53809
53801	53804	53807	53810
53802	53805	53808	

Class 1P 0-4-4T

58086

Class 5 4-6-0

73019	73047	73050	73052
73028	73049	73051	

Class 4 4-6-0

75071	75072	75073

Class 3 2-6-2T

82041

Total 50

Allocations: 1965 (82F)

Class 57xx 0-6-0PT

3681	3758

Class 94xx 0-6-0PT

8436	8486

*The main (ex-SDJR) building at Bath Green Park in
1950 with Class 7F 2-8-0 locos dominating the
metals.* N. E. Preedy

Class 7F 2-8-0 No 53803 (82F) lets off steam outside Bath Green Park in 1960. T. Wright

Class 4F 0-6-0
44558

Class 3F 0-6-0T
47276   47506   47544

Class 8F 2-8-0
48309   48444   48525   48660   48737

Class 5MT 4-6-0
73001   73051   75054   73068

Class 3MT 2-6-2T
82004   82041

Total 19

Bath Green Park shed became Western Region property in 1958 and remained so until closure in March 1966 when that region finished with steam. Whilst not of GWR origin, Bath Green Park and its sister shed at Templecombe became the last two coded steam sheds on the Western Region (see 71H also). As a point of interest, Oxford was the last ex-GWR Western Region shed in steam and closed in January 1966.

A very rare view of the three Fowler 4-4-0s built for the SDJR in 1929 by the LMS. Taken at Bath Green Park in 1929, it depicts the locos with their original numbers, (left to right) 45, 44 and 46. They became LMS Nos 634, 633 and 635 in 1930 and subsequently 40634, 40633 and 40635 upon nationalisation, being withdrawn in 1962, 1959 and 1961 respectively. H. C. Casserley

71H   TEMPLECOMBE

Pre-Grouping Origin: SDJR
Gazetteer Ref: 3 D3
Closed: 1966
Shed-Codes: 22D (1948 to 1950)
71H (1950 to 1958)
82G (1958 to 1963)
83G (1963 to 1966)
Allocations: 1950 (71H)

Class G6 0-6-0T
30274   30277

Class 2P 4-4-0
40509   40563   40564   40634

Class 3P 4-4-0
40741

Class 3F 0-6-0

43194	43218	43248	43593
43216	43228	43356	

Class 4F 0-6-0

44102	44146	44417

Total 17

Allocations: 1959 (82G)

Class 57xx 0-6-0PT
9651

Class 2P 4-4-0
40563   40564   40569   40634

Class 2 2-6-2T
41248

Class 3F 0-6-0

43194	43218	43427
43216	43248	43436

Templecombe shed in 1957 as viewed from the
north.   K. Fairey

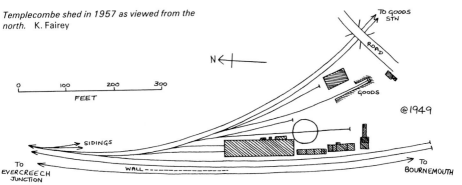

Class 4F 0-6-0
44102 44135 44417 44557

Class 3F 0-6-0T
47542

Class 3 2-6-2T
82039

Total 18

Allocations: 1965 (83G)

Class 2251 0-6-0
3201 3205 3218

Class 57xx 0-6-0PT
4631

Looking north from the rear of Templecombe shed in 1958 with Class 4F 0-6-0 No 44559 (82F) left and '3F' 0-6-0 No 43216 (82G) on the opposite side of the turntable. W. Potter

Class 2P 4-4-0 No 40505 (71G) in early BR livery outside the original wooden shed at Templecombe in 1950. This building was replaced by the brick structure a year later. K. Fairey

Class 2MT 2-6-2T
41208 41214 41243 41296

Class 4MT 4-6-0
75072 75073

Class 4MT 2-6-4T
80043 80059 80067

Total 13

The closure of the ex-SDJR line in March 1966 rendered the shed at Templecombe redundant and all its locos went to scrap (see 71G notes).

As the shed-codes infer, Templecombe was controlled by the Western Region from 1958.

The wooden shed at Templecombe was replaced by a brick structure in 1951.

A close-up study of the rebuilt Templecombe in 1961.   K. Fairey

71I SOUTHAMPTON DOCKS

Pre-Grouping Origin: LSWR
Gazetteer Ref: 4 E4
Closed: 1967
Shed-Codes: 71I (1950 to 1963)
70I (1963 to 1966)
Allocations: 1950 (71I)

Class USA 0-6-0T

30061	30064	30067	30070	30073
30062	30065	30068	30071	30074
30063	30066	30069	30072	

Class E1 0-6-0T

32156	32606

Total 16

Allocations: 1959 (71I)

Class USA 0-6-0T

30061	30064	30067	30070	30073
30062	30065	30068	30071	30074
30063	30066	30069	30072	

Class E2 0-6-0T

32101	32108	32109

Southampton Docks shed from the west in 1949 clearly showing the solitary through lane.   W. Potter

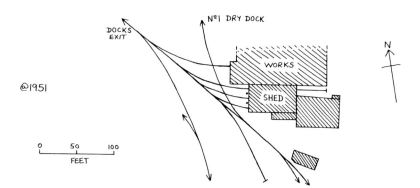

DOCKS
EXIT

Nº1 DRY DOCK

©1951

WORKS

SHED

N

0   50   100
FEET

Class E1 0-6-0T
32151   32689

Total 19

Southampton Docks shed lost its steam allocation to Eastleigh 71A in June 1963 when the last few USA tanks were replaced by diesel shunters. Before the arrival of the USA 0-6-0Ts the most prominent class at the docks were the diminutive Class B4 0-4-0T engines.

Steam continued to use the depot right up to the end of steam power on the Southern Region in July 1967 with locos supplied by Eastleigh. Thus, the Docks became a sub-shed of this depot insofar as steam was concerned. Diesel shunters continued to be allocated in their own right until the official closure of Southampton Docks shed in January 1966, when Eastleigh became the parent depot for both forms of traction.

Often referred to as 'Old Docks' because of the stabling points at New Docks and Southampton Terminus, the shed became known as 'Eastern Docks' from 1965.

The depot was recoded 70I in September 1963 and the shed roof was renewed in 1955.

Class USA 0-6-0Ts are very much in evidence in this 1953 view of Southampton. The roof shown was replaced in 1955.   Real Photographs

This 1960 view of Southampton depicts the shed yard on the right hand side with the rear of Class E2 0-6-0T No 32107 (71J) just visible. Note the tight curves leading into the shed and the rebuilt roof. W. Potter

Southampton Docks in August 1966, seven months after 'official' closure with 'USA' class 0-6-0T No 30067 (70D) and an 0-6-0 diesel shunter. During this period the depot was worked as a sub-shed of Eastleigh 70D (see shed notes). B. J. Ashworth

71J HIGHBRIDGE

Pre-Grouping Origin: SDJR
Gazetteer Ref: 3 B1
Closed: 1966
Shed Codes: 22E (1948 to 1950)
71J (1950 to 1958)
Allocations: 1950 (71J)

Class 3F 0-6-0
43204   43419   43792

Class 1P 0-4-4T
58046   58047   58086   58088

Total 7

At the outset of Highbridge's association with the Southern Region in early 1950 it was ranked as a sub-shed to Templecombe 71H. By the end of the same year it had regained independent status in the form of 71J with the above listed locos as its allocation.

In March 1958 the depot once again found itself without a separate identity as it became sub-shed to 82F Bath Green Park (Highbridge's ex-SDJR sister sheds, Bath Green Park and Templecombe, had become Western Region territory in the previous month).

Although reported closed in May 1959, the shed became a sub-shed to Templecombe 82G (83G from 1963) and usually stabled two locos overnight. The shed building was in a sorry state by 1964, but the depot managed to retain its facilities right up to the end of the SDJR line in March 1966.

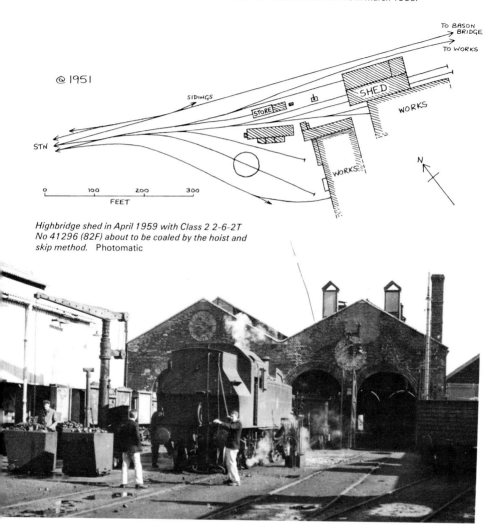

Highbridge shed in April 1959 with Class 2 2-6-2T No 41296 (82F) about to be coaled by the hoist and skip method.   Photomatic

The approaches to Highbridge shed and works as viewed from the west in 1959. Photomatic

Highbridge in July 1960 with Class 3F 0-6-0 No 43194 (82G) seeking attention. During this period the depot was worked as a sub-shed to Templecombe 82G (see shed notes). T. Wright

72A EXMOUTH JUNCTION

Pre-Grouping Origin: LSWR
Gazetteer Ref: 2 B3
Closed: 1965
Shed-Codes: 72A (1950 to 1963)
83D (1963 to 1965)*
Allocations: 1950 (72A)

Class M7 0-4-4T

30024	30046	30133	30256	30377
30025	30049	30245	30320	30668
30030	30055	30252	30323	30669
30034	30105	30253	30374	30671
30039	30124	30255	30376	

Class 02 4-4-4T

30192	30199	30230
30193	30224	30232

Class T9 4-4-0

30283	30703	30707	30716	30723
30702	30706	30715	30717	

Class L11 4-4-0

30408	30409

'King Arthur' 4-6-0
30455 *Sir Launcelot*
30457 *Sir Bedivere*

Class 0395 0-6-0

30564	30581

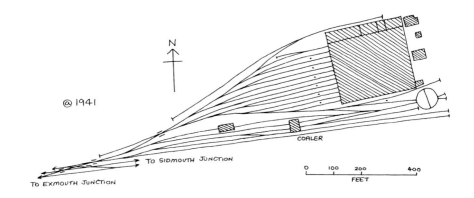

@ 1941

N

CORLER

TO SIDMOUTH JUNCTION

TO EXMOUTH JUNCTION

| 0 | 100 | 200 | | 400 |
FEET

Exmouth Junction shed in 1957 with Classes S15 4-6-0, 'Battle of Britain' and 'West Country' 4-6-2s prominent. R. C. Riley

Class 0415 4-4-2T

| 30582 | 30583 | 30484 |

Class S15 4-6-0

| 30823 | 30825 | 30842 | 30844 | 30846 |
| 30824 | 30841 | 30843 | 30845 | 30847 |

Class Z 0-8-0T

| 30954 |

Class N 2-6-0

31407	31832	31838	31847	31874
31408	31833	31839	31853	31875
31829	31834	31840	31855	
31830	31835	31841	31856	
31831	31837	31845	31869	

Class E1R 0-6-2T

| 32124 | 32135 | 32695 | 32697 |

'West Country' 4-6-2
34001 Exeter
34002 Salisbury
34003 Plymouth
34004 Yeovil
34005 Barnstaple
34006 Bude
34007 Wadebridge
34008 Padstow
34009 Lyme Regis
34010 Sidmouth
34014 Budleigh Salterton
34015 Exmouth
34016 Bodmin
34017 Ilfracombe
34018 Axminster
34019 Bideford
34020 Seaton
34024 Tamar Valley
34025 Rough Tor
34026 Yes Tor
34027 Taw Valley
34028 Eddystone
34029 Lundy
34030 Watersmeet
34031 Torrington
34044 Woolacombe
34045 Ottery St Mary
34046 Braunton
34047 Callington
34048 Crediton

An early BR view of Exmouth Junction shed and coaler seven months after nationalisation.
W. Potter

'Merchant Navy' 4-6-2
35001 *Channel Packet*
35002 *Union Castle*
35003 *Royal Mail*
35004 *Cunard White Star*
35021 *New Zealand Line*
35022 *Holland-America Line*
35023 *Holland-Afrika Line*
35024 *East Asiatic Company*

Total 123

Allocations: 1959 (72A)

Class M7 0-4-4T

30021	30025	30045	30667	30670
30023	30027	30323	30668	30676
30024	30044	30374	30669	

Class 02 0-4-4T

30182	30199	30232

Class 700 0-6-0

30317	30327	30691

Class 0415 4-4-2T

30582	30583	30584

Class T9 4-4-0

30702	30711	30717
30709	30715	30726

Class S15 4-6-0

30841	30843	30845
30842	30844	30846

Class Z 0-8-0T

30950	30953	30955	30956	30957

Class U 2-6-0

31790	31791

Class N 2-6-0

31830	31834	31838	31842	31846
31831	31835	31839	31843	31847
31832	31836	31840	31844	31849
31833	31837	31841	31845	

Class E1R 0-6-2T
32697

'West Country' 4-6-2
34002 *Salisbury*
34011 *Tavistock*
34015 *Exmouth*
34023 *Blackmore Vale*
34024 *Tamar Valley*
34030 *Watersmeet*
34032 *Camelford*
34033 *Chard*
34034 *Honiton*
34035 *Shaftesbury*
34036 *Westward Ho*
34038 *Lynton*
34096 *Trevone*
34104 *Bere Alston*
34106 *Lydford*
34108 *Wincanton*

In this 1963 view of Exmouth (as 83D) Class 64xx 0-6-0PT No 6412 (83D) can be seen on the left.
J. L. Stevenson

'Battle of Britain' 4-6-2
34056 *Croydon*
34057 *Biggin Hill*
34058 *Sir Frederick Pile*
34060 *25 Squadron*
34061 *73 Squadron*
34062 *17 Squadron*
34063 *229 Squadron*
34069 *Hawkinge*
34072 *257 Squadron*
34074 *46 Squadron*
34075 *264 Squadron*
34076 *41 Squadron*
34079 *141 Squadron*
34080 *74 Squadron*
34081 *92 Squadron*
34109 *Sir Trafford Leigh-Mallory*
34110 *66 Squadron*

'Merchant Navy' 4-6-2
35003 *Royal Mail*
35008 *Orient Line*
35009 *Shaw Savill*
35011 *General Steam Navigation*
35013 *Blue Funnel*
35023 *Holland-Afrika Line*
35026 *Lamport & Holt Line*

Class 2 2-6-2T
41306   41307   41318

Class 3 2-6-2T
82010   82013   82018   82022   82024
82011   82017   82019   82023   82025
                                      Total 115

Allocations: 1965 (83D)

Class 57xx 0-6-0PT
4655   4666   4694   9647

Class 2MT 2-6-2T
41206   41223   41291   41317
41216   41249   41307   41321

Class 4MT 4-6-0
75008   75022   75025

Class 4MT 2-6-4T
80037   80041   80064

Class 3MT 2-6-2T
82030   82039   82040   82042   82044
                                      Total 23

*Exmouth Junction shed became part of the Western Region in December 1962 but the shed-code was not given official status until September 1963.

The depot closed in May 1965 and the locos went to Templecombe 83G, Gloucester 85B, Worcester 85A and Bristol Barrow Road 82E.

72B SALISBURY

Pre-Grouping Origin: LSWR
Gazetteer Ref: 4 C5
Closed: 1967
Shed-Codes: 72B (1950 to 1962)
70E (1962 to 1967)
Allocations: 1950 (72B)

Class M7 0-4-4T
30023   30041   30127   30243   30675

Class T9 4-4-0
30122   30289   30709   30724   30727
30288   30301   30719   30725   30730

Class G6 0-6-0T
30238

Class 700 0-6-0
30315   30317   30355   30690   30691

@ 1946

Class L12 4-4-0
30421

'King Arthur' 4-6-0
30448 *Sir Tristram*
30449 *Sir Torre*
30450 *Sir Kay*
30452 *Sir Meliagrance*
30453 *King Arthur*
30454 *Queen Guinevere*
30739 *King Leodegrance*
30744 *Maid of Astolat*
30748 *Vivien*
30753 *Melisande*

STN

TO
YEOVIL

N

```
0    50   100        200        300
                  FEET
```

Salisbury MPD in 1959 with unidentified 'Hall' and
'Castle' class 4-6-0s visiting.   W. Potter

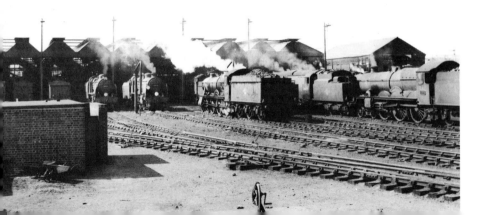

Looking south-west to the Salisbury coaler in 1965 with Class 4MT 4-6-0 No 75077 (70D) alongside. W. Potter

Class 0395 0-6-0
30577

Class S15 4-6-0
30826	30828	30830	30832
30827	30829	30831	

Class Z 0-8-0T
30957

Class U 2-6-0
31612	31618	31626

Class N 2-6-0
31836	31846	31872	31873

'West Country' 4-6-2
34022 *Exmoor*
34023 *Blackmoor Vale*
34032 *Camelford*
34042 *Dorchester*
34043 *Combe Martin*

An overall view of Salisbury shed in 1958 with Southern, Great Western and BR Standard types represented. I. Peters

'Merchant Navy' 4-6-2
35006 *Peninsular & Oriental SN Co*
35007 *Aberdeen Commonwealth*
35008 *Orient Line*
35009 *Shaw Savill*

Total 57

Allocations: 1959 (72B)

Class G6 0-6-0T
30266

Class T9 4-4-0
30301	30313	30729

Class 700 0-6-0
30309	30315	30692

Class H15 4-6-0
30331	30335

'King Arthur' 4-6-0
30448 *Sir Tristram*
30449 *Sir Torre*
30450 *Sir Kay*
30451 *Sir Lamorak*
30452 *Sir Meliagrance*
30453 *King Arthur*

Class M7 0-4-4T
30673	30674

'West Country' class 4-6-2 No 34013 Okehampton (70E) outside Salisbury in 1966. The depot's Pacific classes were reported as being the cleanest in the South Western Division about this time. K. Fairey

Class S15 4-6-0

30823	30826	30829	30832
30824	30827	30830	30847
30825	30828	30831	

Class Z 0-8-0T
30954

Class N 2-6-0
31813   31814

'Battle of Britain' 4-6-2
34049 Anti-Aircraft Command
34050 Royal Observer Corps
34051 Winston Churchill
34052 Lord Dowding
34053 Sir Keith Park
34054 Lord Beaverbrook
34055 Fighter Pilot
34059 Sir Archibald Sinclair

'Merchant Navy' 4-6-2
35004 Cunard White Star
35006 Pensinsular & Oriental SN Co
35007 Aberdeen Commonwealth

Class 4 2-6-0

76005	76006	76007	76008	76009
				Total 47

Allocations: 1965 (70E)

'West Country' 4-6-2
34005 Barnstaple
34006 Bude
34007 Wadebridge
34012 Launceston
34013 Okehampton
34015 Exmouth
34026 Yes Tor
34032 Camelford
34048 Crediton
34100 Appledore
34108 Wincanton

'Battle of Britain' 4-6-2
34051 Winston Churchill
34052 Lord Dowding
34056 Croydon
34057 Biggin Hill
34059 Sir Archibald Sinclair
34063 229 Squadron
34066 Spitfire
34089 602 Squadron

Class 4MT 2-6-0

76005	76007	76008	76017	76067
				Total 24

Closing in July 1967, Salisbury was one of the last seven steam sheds on the Southern Region. The remaining locos went for scrap.

The Western Region had a sub-shed at Salisbury (82D sub) situated nearby North of the running lines. Its closure in November 1950 resulted in the regular appearance of WR stock at the ex-LSWR depot.

72C YEOVIL TOWN

Pre-Grouping Origin: LSWR
Gazetteer Ref: 3E2
Closed: 1965
Shed-Codes: 72C (1950 to 1963)
83E (1963 to 1965)*
Allocations: 1950 (72C)

Class M7 0-4-4T
30058   30129

Class T9 4-4-0
30117   30337   30704   30714

Class L11 4-4-0
30134   30407   30412

Class K10 4-4-0
30389

Class U 2-6-0
31634   31636   31790   31791   31792
                                    Total 15

Allocations: 1959 (72C)

Class 57xx 0-6-0PT
3671   4656   9732
3733   8745   9764

Class 45xx 2-6-2T
5548   5563

Class M7 0-4-4T
30129   30131

Class U 2-6-0
31610   31613   31623   31626   31633
                                    Total 15

Allocations: 1965 (83E)

Class 57xx 0-6-0PT
9670   9754

Class 2MT 2-6-2T
41283   41290

Class 5MT 4-6-0
73166

Class 4MT 4-6-0
75000   75003   75005

Class 4MT 2-6-4T
80039

Class 3MT 2-6-2T
82035
                                    Total 10

The closure of the ex-GWR shed at Yeovil Pen Mill (71H — previously 82E) in January 1959 brought ex-GWR types allocated to Yeovil Town as the lists indicate.

*The depot became part of the Western Region in December 1962 but the shed-code was not given official status until September 1963.

Yeovil Town shed closed in June 1965 and its remaining engines were sent to 83G Templecombe, 85A Worcester and 81F Oxford.

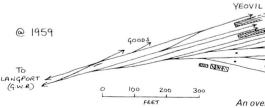

@ 1959

An overall view of Yeovil Town depot in 1957.
Real Photographs

Yeovil Town in 1958 depicting 'King Arthur' class 4-6-0 No 30452 Sir Meliagrance *(72B) on the left hand side.* N. E. Preedy

A busy scene at Yeovil Town in 1957 with 'U' class 2-6-0 No 31790 (72C) facing the camera. H. D. Bowtell

Yeovil Town shed in 1947 as viewed from a nearby field. The station is just visible on the left. LGRP courtesy of David & Charles Ltd

72D PLYMOUTH FRIARY

Pre-Grouping Origin: LSWR
Gazetteer Ref: 1 D5
Closed: 1963
Shed-Codes: 72D (1950 to 1958)
83H (1958 to 1963)
Allocations: 1950 (72D)

Class T1 0-4-4T
30007

Class M7 0-4-4T
30035   30037   30107   30356   30375

Class B4 0-4-0T
30084   30088   30094
30102 *Granville*

Class O2 0-4-4T
30182   30183   30207   30216   30236

Class 757 0-6-2T
30757 *Earl of Mount Edgcumbe*
30758 *Lord St Levan*

Class N 2-6-0
31871

Class E1R 0-6-2T
32094

'West Country' 4-6-2
34011 *Tavistock*
34012 *Launceston*
34013 *Okehampton*
34021 *Dartmoor*

Total 23

Looking west to Plymouth Friary shed from the coaling ramp in 1958. The depot became Western Region territory in this year using the code 83H. Depicted are two of the shed's 'M7' class 0-4-4T locos Nos 30035 and 30034 (both bearing 83H plates). N. E. Preedy

An overall view of Plymouth Friary from the turntable in 1958. 'B4' class 0-4-0T No 30089 of the shed can be seen on the right sandwiched between two coaches. N. E. Preedy

Four named locos at the west end of Plymouth Friary in 1955. left to right are 'Battle of Britain' 4-6-2 No 34069 Hawkinge (72A) '757' 0-6-2T Nos 30758 Lord St Levan, and 30757 Earl of Mount Edgcumbe (both 72D) and 'West Country' 4-6-2 No 34004 Yeovil (72A). The two '757' class locos were a class in their own right and were withdrawn a few years later.   N. E. Preedy

Allocations: 1959 (83H)

Class M7 0-4-4T
30034   30035   30036

Class 02 0-4-4T
30183   30192   30193   30225

Class 2 2-6-2T
41302   41315   41316   41317

Total 11

'West Country' class 4-6-2 No 34011 Tavistock (72D) rests outside the west entrance of Friary shed in 1949.   Real Photographs

Friary shed became Western Region territory in February 1958 as the shed-codes infer.

The depot closed in May 1963 and the four remaining locos (41302, 41315/6/7) transferred to Plymouth Laira 83D.

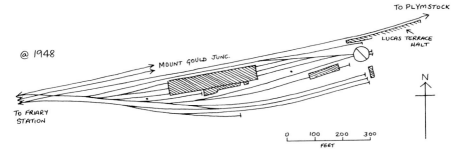

72E BARNSTAPLE JUNCTION

Pre-Grouping Origin: LSWR
Gazetteer Ref: 7 F3
Closed: 1964
Shed-Codes: 72E (1950 to 1963)
83F (1963 to 1964)*
Allocations: 1950 (72E)

Class M7 0-4-4T

30036	30044	30250	30670
30042	30247	30321	

Class N 2-6-0
31842

Class E1R 0-6-2T

32095	32096	32608	32610	32696

Total 13

Allocations: 1959 (72E)

Class M7 0-4-4T

30247	30253	30255	30671
30251	30254	30256	

Class 2 2-6-2T

41294	41295	41297	41298	41314

Total 12

*Barnstaple Junction came under Western Region control in December 1962 but the shed-code was not given official status until September 1963.
The shed closed in September 1964 and the remaining engines went to Exmouth Junction 83D and Templecombe 83G.

Barnstaple shed with a dilapidated roof in the year before closure. The loco facing is 'Battle of Britain' class 4-6-2 No 34065 Hurricane (72A).
J. L. Stevenson

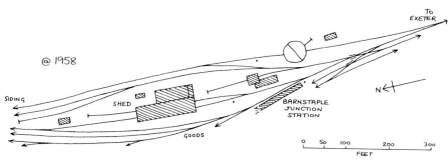

The intact Barnstaple in 1957 with Class 2 2-6-2T No 41294 (72E). The view is that which was obtained from the nearby station platform.   K. Fairey

Barnstaple shed yard and coaling stage in 1952 as viewed from the south. The loco on the right is 'M7' class 0-4-4T No 30253 (72E).   Real Photographs

72F   WADEBRIDGE

Pre-Grouping Origin: LSWR
Gazetteer Ref: 1 C2
Closed: 1964
Shed-Codes: 72F (1950 to 1963)
84E (1963 to 1964)*
Allocations: 1950 (72F)

Class O2 0-4-4T
30200   30203

Class 0298 2-4-0WT
30585   30586   30587

Total 5

Allocations: 1959 (72F)

Class O2 0-4-4T
30200   30236

Class 0298 2-4-0WT
30585   30586   30587

Total 5

*Wadebridge became Western Region property in December 1962 but the shed-code was not given official status until September 1963.

The depot's last engine was withdrawn from service in November 1964.

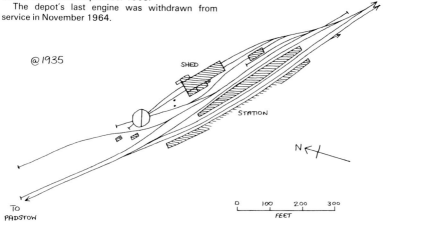

@ 1935

SHED

STATION

N

TO
LAUNCESTON

TO
PADSTOW

0   100   200   300
FEET

An overall view of Wadebridge shed and station from the turntable in 1963.   J. L. Stevenson

Class U 2-6-0 No 31791 (72C) at the north-western end of Wadebridge in 1959.   N. E. Preedy

Wadebridge shed in 1949 depicting Class T9 4-4-0 No 723 (BR 30723) still in Southern livery.
Real Photographs

The south-eastern end of Wadebridge yard with its full complement of Class 0298 2-4-0 well tanks in front of the coaler in 1962. Left to right are Nos 30587, 30586 and 30585.   R. C. Riley

73A   STEWARTS LANE

Pre-Grouping Origin: SECR
Gazetteer Ref: 39 E4
Closed: 1963
Shed-Codes: 73A (1950 to 1962)
75D (1962 to 1963)
Allocations: 1950 (73A)

Class 756 0-6-0T
30756 *A. S. Harris*

'King Arthur' 4-6-0
30763 *Sir Bors de Ganis*
30764 *Sir Gawain*
30766 *Sir Geraint*
30774 *Sir Gaheris*
30775 *Sir Agravaine*
30776 *Sir Galagars*
30778 *Sir Pelleas*
30786 *Sir Lionel*
30793 *Sir Ontzlake*
30796 *Sir Dodinas le Savage*

Class H 0-4-4T

31005	31261	31295	31321
31177	31263	31307	31329
31184	31266	31311	

An elevated view of Stewarts Lane looking west from one of the overhead lines that sandwiched the depot. The year is 1959 and the two segments of roofing nearest the coaler are being replaced.
R. C. Riley

Class E1 4-4-0
31019	31067	31165	31504	31506

Class D1 4-4-0
31145	31487	31743	31749

Class C 0-6-0
31234	31578	31683	31717	31722
31575	31582	31714	31718	
31576	31681	31716	31719	

Class N 2-6-0
31409	31413	31812	31816
31410	31414	31813	31817
31411	31810	31814	31818
31412	31811	31815	31859

Class P 0-6-0T
31555

Class U 2-6-0
31623	31793	31803

Class R 0-4-4T
31660

Class R1 0-4-4T
31706

Class L 4-4-0
31762	31764	31767

Class U1 2-6-0
31903	31905	31907	31909
31904	31906	31908	31910

Class W 2-6-4T
31912	31914	31915

Class E2 0-6-0T
32100	32102	32104	32106
32101	32103	32105	32107

A south-westerly view of Stewarts Lane five months after nationalisation in 1948. W. Potter

Class E1 0-6-0T
32128

'West Country' 4-6-2
34033 Chard
34034 Honiton
34035 Shaftesbury
34091 Weymouth
34092 City of Wells
34101 Hartland
34102 Lapford
34103 Calstock
34104 Bere Alston

A solitary Class W 2-6-4T No 31919 (75C) stands guard at Stewarts Lane in 1961 two years before closure.   J. Oatway

'Battle of Britain' 4-6-2
34066 Spitfire
34067 Tangmere
34068 Kenley
34069 Hawkinge
34070 Manston
34071 601 Squadron
34076 41 Squadron
34083 605 Squadron
34084 253 Squadron
34085 501 Squadron

'Merchant Navy' 4-6-2
35025 Brocklebank Line
35026 Lamport & Holt Line
35027 Port Line
35028 Clan Line

Total 112

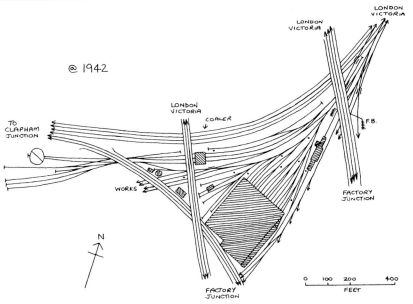

@ 1942

Stewarts Lane shed in 1931 when it was known as 'Longhedge'. At large sheds the increased volumes of smoke made good photography difficult as this view shows. The shed building (far left) is little more than a silhouette as a result.   H. C. Casserley

Allocations: 1959 (73A)

'King Arthur' 4-6-0
30767 Sir Valence
30768 Sir Balin
30769 Sir Balan
30793 Sir Ontzlake
30795 Sir Dinadan
30802 Sir Durnore
30803 Sir Harry le Fise Lake

'Schools' 4-4-0
30908 Westminster
30909 St Paul's
30915 Brighton
30937 Epsom
30938 St Olave's
30939 Leatherhead

Class E1 4-4-0
31019   31067

Class 01 0-6-0
31048   31370

Class D1 4-4-0
31145   31545   31743   31749

Class H 0-4-4T
31261   31265   31550   31551   31552

Class C 0-6-0
31317   31578   31583   31719
31575   31581   31584   31724

Class N 2-6-0
31408   31410   31412   31414   31811
31409   31411   31413   31810   31812

Class P 0-6-0T
31558

Class U1 2-6-0
31894   31897   31904   31906
31895   31898   31905   31907

Class W 2-6-4T
31914   31915   31921

Class E2 0-6-0T
32100   32102   32103   32106

Class C2 0-6-0
32543   32547

'Battle of Britain' 4-6-2
34066 Spitfire
34067 Tangmere
34068 Kenley
34077 603 Squadron
34085 501 Squadron
34086 219 Squadron
34087 145 Squadron
34088 213 Squadron
34089 602 Squadron

'West Country' 4-6-2
34091 Weymouth
34092 City of Wells
34100 Appledore
34101 Hartland

'Merchant Navy' 4-6-2
35001 Channel Packet
35015 Rotterdam Lloyd
35028 Clan Line

Class 2 2-6-2T
41290   41291   41292

Class 4 2-6-4T
42087   42088   42089   42090   42091

Class 5 4-6-0
73041   73080   73082   73084   73086
73042   73081   73083   73085

Class 4 4-6-0
75074

Total 96

Stewarts Lane shed was recoded 75D in June 1962 and survived in this form until closure in September 1963. The remaining engines were transferred to 75A Brighton and 75C Norwood Junction.
     Prior to 1933 the shed was called 'Longhedge' but 'Battersea' was also in common usage.

73B BRICKLAYERS ARMS

Pre-Grouping Origin: SECR
Gazetteer Ref: 40 D4
Closed: 1962
Shed-Code: 73B (1950 to 1962)
Allocations: 1950

'King Arthur' 4-6-0
30794 *Sir Ector de Maris*
30795 *Sir Dinadan*
30798 *Sir Hectimere*
30799 *Sir Ironside*

'Schools' 4-4-0
30908 *Westminster*
30919 *Harrow*
30920 *Rugby*
30921 *Shrewsbury*
30922 *Marlborough*
30923 *Bradfield*
30928 *Stowe*
30929 *Malvern*
30930 *Radley*
30931 *King's Wimbledon*
30932 *Blundells*
30933 *King's Canterbury*
30934 *St Lawrence*
30936 *Cranleigh*
30937 *Epsom*
30938 *St Olave's*
30939 *Leatherhead*

A north-westerly view of the Old shed at Bricklayers Arms in 1960. The locos nearest the camera are (left to right) Class C2 0-6-0 No 32552 (73B), 'U' 2-6-0 No 31638 (70C) and 'Schools' 4-4-0 No 30925 Cheltenham (73B).   W. Potter

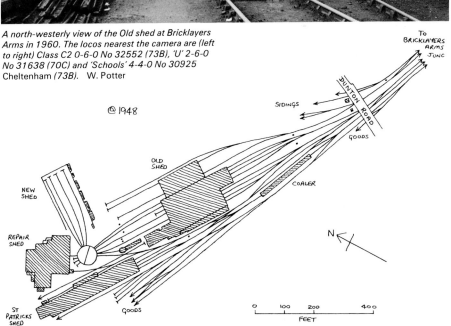

Looking south-east to the Old shed at Bricklayers Arms from the turntable in 1959 with a line of six-coupled classes on view. N. E. Preedy

Class C 0-6-0
31033	31102	31280	31297	31687
31068	31227	31293	31508	31723
31071	31253	31294	31584	31725

Class E 4-4-0
31036	31175	31273	31315	31547
31166	31176	31275	31491	

Class O1 0-6-0
31044	31064	31066	31395

Class E1 4-4-0
31160	31179	31497	31507	31511

Class H 0-4-4T
31162	31324	31533	31544
31278	31326	31541	31546
31309	31500	31542	

Class D 4-4-0
31488	31490	31591	31746

Class L1 4-4-0
31758	31782	31784	31786	31788
31759	31783	31785	31787	31789

Class N 2-6-0
31824	31825	31826	31827

Class U1 2-6-0
31901	31902

Class I1X 4-4-2T
32008	32596	32602

Class B4 4-4-0
32050	32056	32070

Class E1 0-6-0T
32113	32151

Class E3 0-6-2T
32165	32168	32453	32459	32461
32166	32170	32458	32460	32462

Class E6 0-6-2T
32408	32410	32412	32413	32415

Class C2 0-6-0
32442	32448	32525	32551
32446	32524	32549	32554

Class E4 0-6-2T
32463	32469	32474	32499	32565
32467	32472	32481	32564	

'West Country' class 4-6-2 No 34014 Budleigh Salterton *(73B) peers outside Bricklayers Arms in 1961.* T. Wright

Class E5 0-6-2T
32585   32587   32590

Class WD 2-8-0
90164   90226   90375   90552
90194   90234   90408   90558
90216   90254   90533   90564
                                    Total 140

Allocations: 1959

'King Arthur' 4-6-0
30799 Sir Ironside
30800 Sir Meleaus de Lile

'Schools' 4-4-0
30924 Haileybury
30925 Cheltenham
30926 Repton
30927 Clifton
30928 Stowe
30929 Malvern
30930 Radley
30931 King's Wimbledon
30932 Blundells
30933 King's Canterbury
30934 St Lawrence
30935 Sevenoaks
30936 Cranleigh

Class C 0-6-0
31068   31086   31267   31480
31071   31102   31293   31717

Class D1 4-4-0
31247   31735   31739   31741

Class H 0-4-4T
31305   31306   31533   31540   31553

Class E1 4-4-0
31497   31507

Another view of the south-east end of Bricklayers Arms with Class N 2-6-0 No 31866 (75B) to the fore. J. Bentley Collection

Class L1 4-4-0
31783   31784

Class N 2-6-0
31823   31826   31829   31870   31873
31824   31827   31851   31871   31874
31825   31828   31853   31872   31875

Class U1 2-6-0
31890   31899   31901
31891   31900   31902

Class E2 0-6-0T
32104   32105   32107

Class E6 0-6-2T
32408   32410   32415   32417   32418

Class E4 0-6-2T
32471   32473   32557   32565
32472   32474   32564

Class C2 0-6-0
32525   32539   32552   32554
32538   32551   32553

'West Country' 4-6-2
34001 Exeter
34003 Plymouth
34004 Yeovil
34005 Barnstaple
34012 Launceston
34013 Okehampton
34014 Budleigh Salterton

Class 2 2-6-2T
41299   41300   41301   41303

Class 4 -2-6-4T
42080   42081   42082   42086
                                    Total 94

Bricklayers Arms shed dealt mostly with freight turns situated as it was amid the extensive Bricklayers Arms Goods Yard.

Upon closure in June 1962 the remaining engines were transferred to Stewarts Lane 75D, Norwood Junction 75C and Brighton 75A.

73C   HITHER GREEN

Origin: Southern Railway (1933)
Gazetteer Ref: 40 E3
Closed: 1961
Shed-Code: 73C (1950 to 1961)
Allocations: 1950

'King Arthur' 4-6-0
30800 Sir Meleaus de Lile

Class C 0-6-0
31018	31061	31270	31581	31695
31054	31150	31480	31689	31720
31059	31245	31486	31694	

Class E 4-4-0
31159

Class O1 0-6-0
31248	31258	31391	31432

Class U 2-6-0
31616	31617	31639

Class D 4-4-0
31732

Class N1 2-6-0
31822	31877	31879
31876	31878	31880

Class W 2-6-4T
31911	31921	31923	31925
31913	31922	31924	

Class WD 2-8-0
90107	90213	90390	90669	90702
90127	90267	90556	90671	90718
90142	90389	90566	90678	

Total 51

Allocations: 1959

'King Arthur' 4-6-0
30796 Sir Dodinas le Savage
30806 Sir Galleron

A head on view of Hither Green shed in 1957.
J. A. Peden

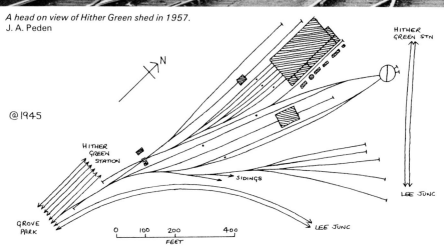

Class C 0-6-0			
31033	31287	31688	31692	31721
31054	31498	31689	31693	31725
31061	31573	31690	31694	
31253	31686	31691	31695	

Class N1 2-6-0		
31822	31877	31879
31876	31878	31880

Class N 2-6-0			
31855	31857	31859	31861
31856	31858	31860	

An overall view of Hither Green shed a few months before closure in 1961 with diesel power well established. K. Fairey

Two of Hither Green's Class C 0-6-0s Nos 31268 and 31721 are in the foreground of this 1960 view of the depot. N. E. Preedy

Class W 2-6-4T			
31911	31913	31922	31924
31912	31916	31923	31925

Class Q1 0-6-0			
33014	33037	33039	33040

Total 45

Hither Green lost the bulk of its allocation in May 1961, but the last three locos (31686/89/90) went to Ashford 73F and Bricklayers Arms 73B at closure in October the same year.

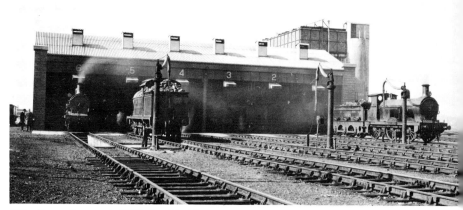

Hither Green when new in 1933. Ian Allan Library

73D GILLINGHAM

Pre-Grouping Origin: SECR
Gazetteer Ref: 6 B5
Closed: 1960
Shed-Code: 73D (1950 to 1959)
Allocations: 1950

Class Z 0-8-0T
30951

Class C 0-6-0

31086	31225	31317	31583	31693
31090	31255	31498	31585	31712
31112	31256	31510	31588	31713
31221	31267	31573	31682	31724
31223	31287	31579	31688	

Class D 4-4-0
31092   31729

Class H 0-4-4T
31308

Class D1 4-4-0
31492   31494

Class E 4-4-0
31516

Class R 0-4-4T

31658	31662	31665
31659	31663	31666

Class R1 0-4-4T
31697

Total 38

Allocations: 1959

Class C 0-6-0

31037	31229	31510	31682	31720
31112	31297	31576	31683	
31227	31495	31579	31684	

Class H 0-4-4T

31161	31322	31518
31308	31512	31548

Class L1 4-4-0
31785   31786   31787

Class N 2-6-0
31815   31816

Total 24

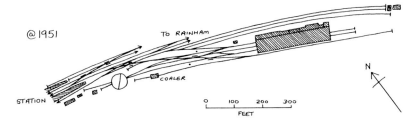

The north-western end of Gillingham shed in 1958.
R. C. Riley

This 1958 view of the south-eastern end of Gillingham shows track alterations in progress with Class L1 4-4-0 No 31786 (73D) as overseer.
R. C. Riley

Gillingham lost its allocation in May 1959 to the following depots: Nine Elms 70A, Brighton 75A, Dover 73H and Hither Green 73C. From this date it became a sub-shed to Ashford 73F yet curiously operated with locos from Tonbridge 73J.

The depot finally closed in June 1960.

The coaling stage at Gillingham in the month the depot lost its allocation, May 1959. Locos left to right are Classes L1 4-4-0 No 31786 (73D), 'C' 0-6-0 No 31297 (73D) and 'L' 4-4-0 No 31779 (73G). The two former locos transferred to Nine Elms 70A. R. C. Riley

Class L 4-4-0 No 31780 (74B) and 'C' Class 0-6-0 No 31229 (73D) outside the north-western end of Gillingham in 1955. D. T. Rowe

73E FAVERSHAM

Pre-Grouping Origin: SECR
Gazetteer Ref: 6 C3
Closed: 1959
Shed-Codes: 73E (1950 to 1959)
Allocations: 1950

Class E 4-4-0
31157

Class C 0-6-0

31229	31268	31495	31692
31242	31481	31691	31715

Class 01 0-6-0
31369

Faversham in 1957 with Class 2 2-6-2T No 41313 (73E) and 'Schools' 4-4-0 No 30930 Radley (73B) facing. Photomatic

Class D1 4-4-0

31489	31505	31739
31502	31727	31741

Class D 4-4-0

31501	31586	31734

Class U 2-6-0

31631	31638	31806	31808

Class R 0-4-4T

31661	31674

Class R1 0-4-4T

31696	31698	31705

Class N 2-6-0

31850	31854	31868

Total 31

Allocations: 1959

Class C 0-6-0

31242	31256	31298	31714
31255	31268	31481	31715

Class D1 4-4-0

31494	31505	31509

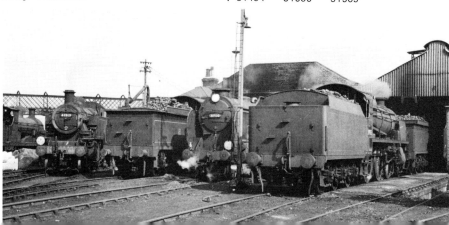

Class H 0-4-4T
31503

Class L 4-4-0
31765   31766   31768

Class N 2-6-0
31850   31852

Class U1 2-6-0
31892   31893   31903

Class 2 2-6-2T
41308   41310   41312
41309   41311   41313

Total 26

A variety of Southern classes outside Faversham in 1934. The original structure is on the right and was reroofed a year later whilst the left hand building survived in this form until the early 1950s when it too was refurbished.   H. C. Casserley

Faversham shed closed in June 1959 and the locos were dispersed to no fewer than seven depots: Nine Elms 70A, Ashford 73F, Dover 73H, Feltham 70B, Exmouth Junction 72A, Stewarts Lane 73A and Tonbridge 73J.

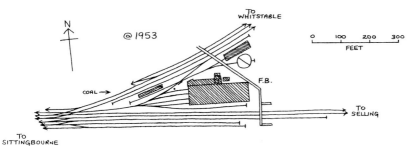

Looking south-east to the remains of Faversham in 1963, four years after closure.   M. S. Houlgrave

74A ASHFORD

Origin: Southern Railway (1931)
Gazetteer Ref: 6 D3
Closed: 1963
Shed-Codes: 74A (1950 to 1958)
73F (1958 to 1963)
Allocations: 1950 (74A)

Class B4 0-4-0T
30096 *Normandy*

'King Arthur' 4-6-0
30797 *Sir Blamor de Ganis*
30801 *Sir Meliot de Logres*
30802 *Sir Durnore*
30803 *Sir Harry le Fise Lake*
30804 *Sir Cador of Cornwall*
30805 *Sir Constantine*

Class Z 0-8-0T
30953

Class R1 0-6-0T

31010	31069	31339

Class 01 0-6-0

31041	31370	31379

Class H 0-4-4T

31158	31239	31274	31322
31161	31269	31305	31520

Class C 0-6-0

31218	31271	31572	31711
31260	31513	31589	31721

Class N 2-6-0

31400	31402	31404	31406	31861
31401	31403	31405	31860	

Class D 4-4-0

31477	31574	31577	31748

Class E 4-4-0
31514

Class J 0-6-4T

31595	31596	31597	31598

Class S 0-6-0ST
31685

Class R1 0-4-4T
31710

Class D1 4-4-0
31736

Class L 4-4-0

31763	31771	31773	31775
31770	31772	31774	

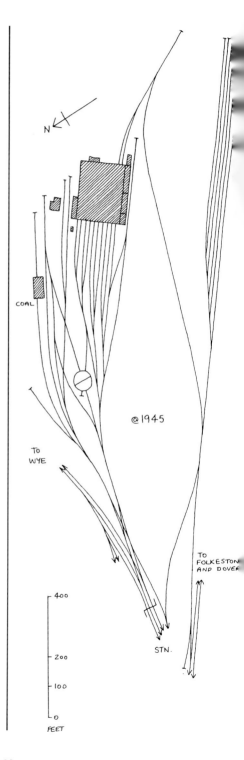

68

A south-easterly view of Ashford shed in 1952 with many different classes on display. B. K. B. Green

Class A1X 0-6-0T

32640	32644	32659	32670	32678
				Total 63

Allocations: 1959 (73F)

Class Z 0-8-0T

30951	30952

Class H 0-4-4T

31005	31276	31319	31520
31263	31307	31519	31522

Class C 0-6-0

31218	31219	31221	31223	21589

Class D1 4-4-0

31246	31727

Class N 2-6-0

31400	31402	31404	31406	31848
31401	31403	31405	31407	31854

Class D1 4-4-0 No 31745 (74D) still bearing Southern markings stands near the coaler at Ashford in 1949. Real Photographs

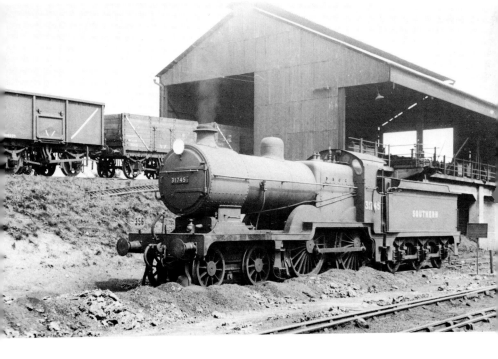

Ashford shed during a visit by members of the RCTS in March 1962, 18 months before closure with diesels dominating the metals.   K. Fairey

Ashford shed was recoded 73F in October 1958 and survived in this form until October 1963 when the depot closed to steam. The only remaining locos were three 'C' class engines which Ashford Works utilised for shunting purposes. The bulk of the allocation departed in mid-1962 for Exmouth Junction 72A, Stewarts Lane 75D and Three Bridges 75E.

Class L1 4-4-0
| 31756 | 31757 | 31758 | 31759 | 31782 |

Class A1X 0-6-0T
32636

Class 4 2-6-4T
| 42096 | 42097 | 42098 | 42099 | 42100 |

Class 2 2-6-2T
| 84020 | 84021 | 84022 | 84023 | 84024 |
| | | | | Total 43 |

Ashford Works was quite near the shed and part of its function was the scrapping of withdrawn locos. Here we see 'Schools' class 4-4-0 No 30909 St Paul's (withdrawn from 70C in February 1962) partly cut up in March 1962 (see Reading view).   K. Fairey

74B RAMSGATE

Origin: Southern Railway (1930)
Gazetteer Ref: 6 B1
Closed: 1960
Shed-Codes: 74B (1950 to 1958)
73G (1958 to 1959)
Allocations: 1950 (74B)

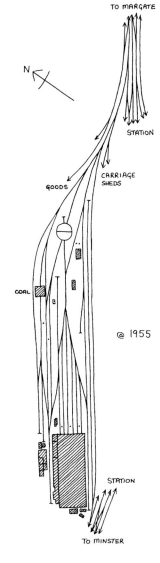

TO MARGATE

N

STATION

CARRIAGE
SHEDS

GOODS

COAL

B

@ 1955

STATION

TO MINSTER

0   100   200   400

FEET

'Schools' 4-4-0
30911 *Dover*
30912 *Downside*
30913 *Christ's Hospital*
30914 *Eastbourne*
30915 *Brighton*
30916 *Whitgift*
30917 *Ardingly*
30918 *Hurstpierpoint*

Class C 0-6-0
31004   31252   31298   31592   31690

Class 01 0-6-0
31065   31093   31390

Class H 0-4-4T
31259   31519   31522   31543
31265   31521   31532

Class L 4-4-0
31776   31777   31780   31781

'Battle of Britain' 4-6-2
34077 *603 Squadron*
34078 *222 Squadron*
34079 *141 Squadron*
34080 *74 Squadron*
34081 *92 Squadron*
34082 *615 Squadron*
34086 *219 Squadron*
34087 *145 Squadron*
34088 *213 Squadron*
34089 *602 Squadron*
34090 *66 Squadron*

'West Country' 4-6-2
34096 *Trevone*
34097 *Holsworthy*
34098 *Templecombe*
34099 *Lynmouth*
34100 *Appledore*

Total 43

Allocations: 1959 (73G)

'Schools' 4-4-0
30910 *Merchant Taylors*
30911 *Dover*
30912 *Downside*
30913 *Christ's Hospital*
30914 *Eastbourne*
30916 *Whitgift*
30917 *Ardingly*
30918 *Hurstpierpoint*
30919 *Harrow*
30920 *Rugby*
30921 *Shrewsbury*
30922 *Marlborough*

Class C 0-6-0
31004   31245   31252   31271   31592

Class H 0-4-4T
31324   31326   31500

Looking west to Ramsgate shed in 1958 with
'Schools' 4-4-0 No 30915 Brighton (73A) and 'King
Arthur' 4-6-0 No 30803 Sir Harry le Fise Lake (74A)
left and right respectively.   H. C. Casserley

Ramsgate from the coaling plant in Southern Days.
Ian Allan Library

A 1960 view of the water softener at Ramsgate
when the depot had been reduced to a sub-shed of
Ashford 73F. Note the prefabricated structure on the
left which was erected for the coming of the EMUs.
R. C. Riley

Various 4-4-0 classes at Ramsgate in 1927.
H. C. Casserley

Class L 4-4-0
31764   31775   31779   31780   31781

'West Country' 4-6-2
34016 *Bodmin*
34017 *Ilfracombe*
34021 *Dartmoor*
34022 *Exmoor*
34025 *Whimple*
34026 *Yes Tor*
34027 *Taw Valley*
34037 *Clovelly*

'Battle of Britain' 4-6-2
34078 *222 Squadron*

Class 2 2-6-2T
84025   84026   84027   84028   84029
                                  Total 39

Ramsgate lost its allocation in June 1959 when it became sub-shed to Ashford 73F. The locos transferred to Nine Elms 70A, Bricklayers Arms 73B, Ashford 73F, Dover 73H, Stewarts Lane 73A and Brighton 75A.
     Final closure came in December 1960.

74C   DOVER

Origin: Southern Railway (1928)
Gazetteer Ref: 6 D2
Closed: 1961
Shed-Codes: 74C (1950 to 1958)
73H (1958 to 1961)
Allocations: 1950 (74C)

'King Arthur' 4-6-0
30767 *Sir Valence*
30768 *Sir Balin*
30769 *Sir Balan*
30770 *Sir Prianius*
30771 *Sir Sagramore*
30781 *Sir Aglovale*
30806 *Sir Galleron*

'Schools' 4-4-0
30924 *Haileybury*
30925 *Cheltenham*
30926 *Repton*
30927 *Clifton*

Class P 0-6-0T
31027   31323   31557   31558

Class R1 0-6-0T
31047   31128   31154   31340
31107   31147   31337

Class O1 0-6-0
31048   31373   31383   31430
31108   31381   31425   31434

Class C 0-6-0
31063   31113   31191   31243   31291

Class D1 4-4-0
31247   31470   31545   31735

Class H 0-4-4T
31276   31503   31518   31531
31306   31512   31530   31540

Class R 0-4-4T
31673

Class R1 0-4-4T
31708

Class D 4-4-0
31737

Class L1 4-4-0
31753   31754   31755   31756   31757

Class N 2-6-0
31819   31820   31821   31823

Class E2 0-6-0T
32108   32109

Class D1 0-4-2T
32359

'Battle of Britain' 4-6-2
34072 *257 Squadron*
34073 *249 Squadron*
34074 *46 Squadron*
34075 *264 Squadron*

'Merchant Navy' 4-6-2
35029 *Ellerman Lines*
35030 *Elder Dempster Lines*

Total 68

Allocations: 1959 (73H)

Class 57xx 0-6-0PT
4601   4616   4630
4610   4626   4631

Class B4 0-4-0T
30084

'King Arthur' 4-6-0
30775 *Sir Agravaine*
30777 *Sir Lamiel*
30797 *Sir Blamor de Ganis*
30798 *Sir Hectimere*
30804 *Sir Cador of Cornwall*
30805 *Sir Constantine*

Class R1 0-6-0T
31010   31107   31174
31047   31128   31337

Class P 0-6-0T
31027   31323

Class 01 0-6-0
31065   31258   31425   31430   31434

Class C 0-6-0
31113   31150   31191   31243

Class H 0-4-4T
31328   31542

Class L1 4-4-0
31753   31754   31755   31788   31789

Class N 2-6-0
31818   31819   31820   31821

'Battle of Britain' 4-6-2
34070 *Manston*
34071 *601 Squadron*
34073 *249 Squadron*
34082 *615 Squadron*
34083 *605 Squadron*
34084 *253 Squadron*

'West Country' 4-6-2
34103 *Calstock*

Class 4 2-6-4T
42074   42076   42078   42092
42075   42077   42079   42095

Class 4 4-6-0
75065   75066   75067   75068   75069

Total 61

DOVER MARINE STN

400

200

100

0

FEET

DOVER PRIORY STN

@ 1948

N

TO ARCHCLIFFE JUNCTION

Dover was re-coded 73H in October 1958 and remained so until closure in October 1961. The displaced locos transferred to Salisbury 72B, Nine Elms 70A and Stewarts Lane 73A.

The shed was sometimes referred to as 'Marine'.

Looking west to Dover Marine shed from the coaler in 1949. The locos in the centre of the view are 'King Arthur' 4-6-0 No 30768 Sir Balin *and 'Schools' 4-4-0 No 30924* Haileybury *(both 74C).*
Real Photographs

An overall view of Dover in 1959 from the direction of Marine station. R. C. Riley

The original ex-SECR shed at Dover Priory in 1927. This four lane depot declined in importance with the opening of the Southern Marine shed in 1928, but nevertheless managed to survive until 1932.
H. C. Casserley

74D TONBRIDGE

Pre-Grouping Origin: SECR
Gazetteer Ref: 5 D5
Closed: 1965
Shed-Codes: 74D (1950-1958)
73J (1958 to 1962)
Allocations: 1950 (74D)

Class H 0-4-4T

31164	31320	31517	31548
31193	31327	31523	31550

Class C 0-6-0

31219	31272	31461	31590	31684
31244	31277	31580	31593	31686

Class D1 4-4-0

31246	31509	31745

Class D 4-4-0

31496	31728	31731
31549	31730	31733

Class R 0-4-4T

31667	31670	31671	31675

Class R1 0-4-4T

31700	31703	31704

Class L 4-4-0

31760	31761	31765	31778	31779

Class E1 0-6-0T
32145

Class E3 0-6-2T

32167	32169	32454	32456

The western end of Tonbridge shed in 1957.
R. Blencowe

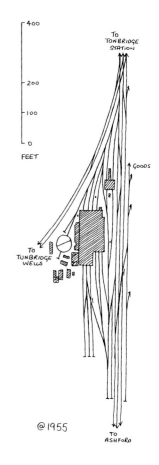

@ 1955

Looking across the Tonbridge and Tunbridge Wells line to the coaler at Tonbridge in 1961 with Class H 0-4-4T No 31543 (75F) in front of the canopy.
R. C. Riley

A close up of Tonbridge in 1961 from the west.
R. C. Riley

Class E4 0-6-2T

32488	32503	32580	32581

Class Q1 0-6-0

33026	33029	33032	33035	33038
33027	33030	33033	33036	
33028	33031	33034	33037	

Total 61

Allocations: 1959 (73J)

Class H 0-4-4T

31164	31239	31279	31523
31177	31259	31295	31543
31193	31266	31517	

Class C 0-6-0

31244	31272	31588	31716
31270	31280	31590	

Class D1 4-4-0

31470	31487	31489	31492

Class L 4-4-0

31760	31763	31771
31762	31770	31773

The eastern end of Tonbridge depot in 1962, a few months before its demotion to sub of Stewarts Lane 75D. K. Fairey

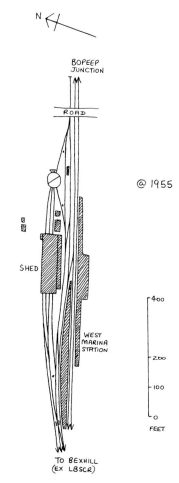

Class U1 2-6-0
31896   31908   31909   31910

Class E3 0-6-2T
32456

Class E4 0-6-2T
32578   32580

Class Q1 0-6-0
33024   33029   33031   33033   33035
33028   33030   33032   33034   33036
Total 45

Tonbridge shed was recoded 73J in October 1958 and remained so until June 1962 when it was demoted to sub-shed of Stewarts Lane 75D. The engines transferred to Exmouth Junction 72A, Stewarts Lane 75D and Eastleigh 71A. However, when Stewarts Lane closed in September 1963, Tonbridge found itself sub-shedded to Redhill 75B. It survived in this form until closure in January 1965 when its remaining locos went to Tunbridge Wells West, itself a sub-shed of Redhill 75B by this time.

The shed was re-roofed in 1952.

74E   ST LEONARDS

Pre-Grouping Origin: LBSCR
Gazetteer Ref: 6 F5
Closed: 1958
Shed-Code: 74E (1950 to 1958)
Allocations: 1950 (74E)

N

BOPEEP JUNCTION

ROAD

@ 1955

SHED

WEST MARINA STATION

400

200

100

0

FEET

TO BEXHILL
(EX LBSCR)

'Schools' 4-4-0
30900 *Eton*
30901 *Winchester*
30902 *Wellington*
30903 *Charterhouse*
30904 *Lancing*
30905 *Tonbridge*
30906 *Sherborne*
30907 *Dulwich*
30909 *St Paul's*
30910 *Merchant Taylors*
30935 *Sevenoaks*

A diminutive Class A1X 0-6-0T No 32670 (74E) stands before an unidentified 'Schools' class 4-4-0 at St Leonards in 1957. K. Fairey

St Leonards shed from the west in 1952 with (left to right) 'Schools' 4-4-0 No 30937 Epsom *(73B), 'C' 0-6-0 No 31038 (74E) and 'D3' 0-4-4T No 32386 (75A).* Real Photographs

Class C 0-6-0
31037   31038

Class R1 0-6-0T
31174   31335

Class H 0-4-4T
31279   31310   31319   31328

Class D 4-4-0
31493   31738

Class E 4-4-0
31587

Class L 4-4-0
31766   31768   31769

Class D3 0-4-4T
32378   32388   32391

An overall view of the eastern end of St Leonards in 1950 with West Marina station to the left of the depot.
LGRP courtesy of David & Charles Ltd

Class Q1 0-6-0
33039   33040

Total 30

St Leonards shed from the east in 1963, five years after closure. The brightness of the rail surface leading to and on the turntable would suggest that the site was still in use as a turning point. However, the presence of the canopied fuel pump would cause diesel power to contribute to this.   K. Fairey

St Leonards shed lost its allocation in June 1958 with the bulk of the engines going to Tonbridge 74D, Ashford 74A, Brighton 75A and Tunbridge Wells West 75F. Although the depot continued to service the odd visitor after this date, it is safe to regard the shed as being closed in that month.

75A BRIGHTON

Pre-Grouping Origin: LBSCR
Gazetteer Ref: 5 F3
Closed: 1964
Shed-Code: 75A (1950 to 1964)
Allocations: 1950

Class P 0-6-0T
31178   31556

Class U1 2-6-0
31890   31891   31892   31893   31894

Class I1X
32005   32595

Class H1 4-4-2
32037   32038   32039

Class I3 4-4-2T
32076   32086   32088

Class E1 0-6-0T
32139   32142   32689

Class K 2-6-0
32337   32341   32343   32345   32347
32339   32342   32344   32346   32349

A bird's eye view of Brighton shed in 1958 with many different classes represented.   T. Wright

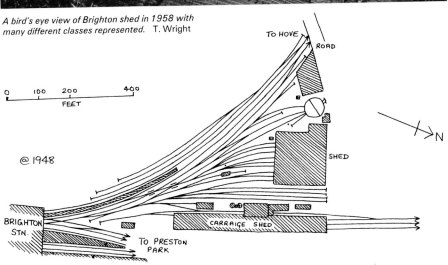

Brighton as viewed from the station platform in 1963. Nearest the camera is Class 2MT 2-6-2T No 41301 (75A). K. Fairey

Class D3 0-4-4T

32368	32372	32376	32386	32393

Class E5 0-6-2T

32400	32575	32583
32573	32576	32594

Class H2 4-4-2T
32421 *South Foreland*
32422 *North Foreland*
32424 *Beachy Head*
32425 *Trevose Head*
32426 *St Albans Head*

Class C2 0-6-0

32437	32443	32528	32543
32438	32523	32539	

Class E3 0-6-2T
32455

Class E4 0-6-2T

32470	32486	32505	32513	32577
32471	32494	32508	32514	
32475	32504	32509	32566	

Looking east across the shed yard at Brighton in 1963 with Class A1X 0-6-0T No 32640 (75A) in the foreground. R. C. Riley

Class A1X 0-6-0T
32636   32647

'West Country' 4-6-2
34036 Westward Ho
34037 Clovelly
34038 Lynton
34039 Boscastle
34040 Crewkerne
34041 Wilton

Class WD 2-8-0
90247   90354

Total 75

Allocations: 1959

Class M7 0-4-4T
30031   30053   30056   30110
30052   30055   30109

'Schools' 4-4-0
30900 Eton
30901 Winchester

Class P 0-6-0T
31325   31556

Class L 4-4-0
31776   31777   31778

Class K 2-6-0
32338   32340   32342
32339   32341   32343

Class C2 0-6-0
32441   32442   32449

Class E4 0-6-2T
32468   32484   32504   32515   32577
32475   32494   32508   32519
32480   32503   32512   32562

Class A1X 0-6-0T
32635   32655   32662   32670

'West Country' 4-6-2
34008 Padstow
34019 Bideford
34097 Holsworthy
34098 Templecombe
34099 Lynmouth

Class 4 2-6-4T
42066   42067

Class 4 4-6-0
75070

Class 4 2-6-4T
80013   80033   80147   80150   80153
80031   80145   80148   80151   80154
80032   80146   80149   80152

Total 62

Brighton shed closed in June 1964 and the last few engines transferred to Bournemouth 70F and Guildford 70C. Despite closure, the shed received the odd steam visitor well into 1965.

The westerly side of Brighton shed with the lines to Hove visible on the left.   K. Fairey

75B REDHILL

Pre-Grouping Origin: SECR
Gazetteer Ref: 5 C3
Closed: 1965
Shed-Code: 75B (1950 to 1965)
Allocations: 1950

Class N 2-6-0
31843	31849	31857	31863
31844	31851	31858	31864
31848	31852	31862	31865

Class U1 2-6-0
31895	31897	31899
31896	31898	31900

Class C2 0-6-0
32449	32450	32540	32541	32550

Class E4 0-6-2T
32507	32517	32560	32561

Class E5 0-6-2T
32592

Class WD 2-8-0
90317	90360	90641

Total 31

Allocations: 1959

Class S15 4-6-0
30835	30836	30837

Class N 2-6-0
31817	31863	31865	31867	31869
31862	31864	31866	31868	

Class C2 0-6-0
32450	32451

Class 4 2-6-0
76053	76055	76057	76059	76061
76054	76056	76058	76060	76062

Total 24

Allocations: 1965

Class N 2-6-0
31405

Redhill shed and coaler from the north in 1964.
W. Potter

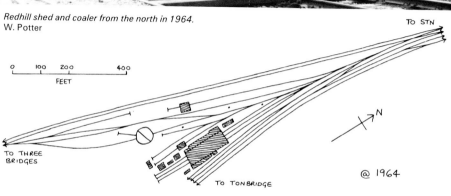

0   100   200   400
FEET

TO STN

N

TO THREE BRIDGES

TO TONBRIDGE

@ 1964

84

Class 4MT 2-6-4T				
80011	80034	80088	80141	80151
80019	80068	80089	80142	80152
80032	80084	80094	80144	
80033	80085	80140	80145	

Total 19

Redhill closed in June 1965 and was the last Central Division depot in steam. The majority of the locos transferred to Feltham 70B and Salisbury 70E.

The southern end of Redhill in 1959 from an elevated viewpoint. The two locos nearest the camera are Class 'C' 0-6-0 No 31245 and 'D1' 4-4-0 No 31247, evidently in store as their covered chimneys suggest.   J. L. Stevenson

Redhill (north end) from a different viewpoint in 1963 with (left to right) Classes U 2-6-0 No 31617 (70A) and N 2-6-0 No 31411 (75B) facing the shed.   K. Fairey

Looking north-west to Redhill's turntable in 1960 with the town in the distance. Two of the depot's Class N 2-6-0s are on show namely No 31868 (left) and 31817.   J. C. Beckett

75C NORWOOD JUNCTION

Origin: Southern Railway (1935)
Gazetteer Ref: 40 G4
Closed: 1964
Shed-Code: 75C (1950 to 1964)
Allocations: 1950

Class Q 0-6-0

30533	30537	30539
30534	30538	30547

Class W 2-6-4T

31916	31917	31918	31919	31920

Class E6 0-6-2T

32407	32411	32416	32418
32409	32414	32417

Class C2 0-6-0

32440	32447	32535	32546
32444	32526	32536	32547

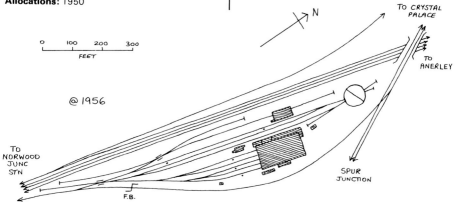

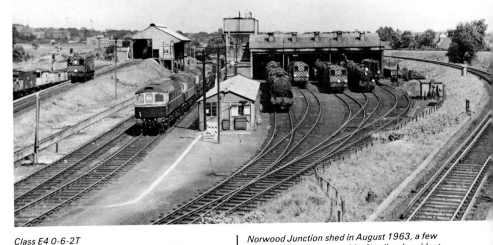

Class E4 0-6-2T
32466	32477	32489	32502
32473	32478	32495	32506
32476	32479	32498	32578

Total 38

Allocations: 1959

Class Q 0-6-0
30533	30537	30540
30534	30538	30549

Class W 2-6-4T
| 31917 | 31918 | 31919 | 31920 |

Norwood Junction shed in August 1963, a few months before closure with nine diesels evident amongst the 17 locos visible. J. Scrace

Norwood Junction on the occasion of a society visit in 1958. Photomatic

Class E3 0-6-2T
32165   32166

Class E6 0-6-2T
32416

Class C2 0-6-0

32443	32445	32447	32521	32545
32444	32446	32448	32544	32546
				Total 23

Most of Norwood Junction's allocation was transferred away in December 1963 but the last few locos were withdrawn upon closure in January 1964.

Looking north-east to Norwood from the ash roads in 1957. Photomatic

A busy scene at Norwood Junction in April 1960. K. Fairey

75D HORSHAM

Pre-Grouping Origin: LBSCR
Gazetteer Ref: 5 E2
Closed: 1964
Shed-Code: 75D (1950 to 1959)
Allocations: 1950

Class M7 0-4-4T
30027   30047

Class Q 0-6-0
30545   30546

Class C3 0-6-0
32302

Class D3 0-4-4T
32364   32365   32379   32380   32384

Class E5 0-6-2T
32399   32401   32568   32570   32586

Class E4 0-6-2T
32464   32501   32515
32482   32511   32556

Class C2 0-6-0
32521   32537   32544   32548

Total 25

Allocations: 1959

Class M7 0-4-4T
30047   30048   30049   30050   30051

Class Q 0-6-0
30544   30545   30546   30547

An overall view of Horsham roundhouse in 1959
with Class E4 0-6-2T No 32475 (75A) alongside a
water column.   J. Scrace

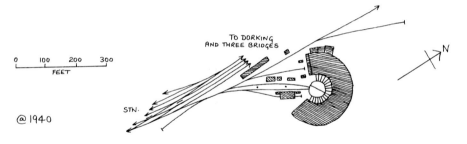

0   100   200   300
FEET

TO DORKING
AND THREE BRIDGES

N

STN.

@ 1940

Class E4 0-6-2T
32463   32469   32470

Class C2 0-6-0
32522   32526   32541

Total 15

Two views of the same locomotive, Class E4 0-6-2T No 32470 (75D) in different years at Horsham. The exterior view shows the loco on the turntable in 1958 (Photomatic) whilst the interior 1961 shot gives a good full length perspective in relation to the size of the stabling radii. T. Wright

Horsham became a sub-shed of Three Bridges 75E in July 1959 and lost its allocation to Three Bridges 75E and Brighton 75A. The closure of Three Bridges in January 1964 resulted in Horsham being worked as a sub-shed of Brighton 75A until its own demise in June of the same year.

The sorry sight at Horsham after closure with headless water column and redundant coal stage.
T. Wright

75E   THREE BRIDGES

Pre-Grouping Origin: LBSCR
Gazetteer Ref: 5 D3
Closed: 1964
Shed-Code: 75E (1950 to 1964)
Allocations: 1950

Class Q 0-6-0
30540   30541

Class I1X 4-4-2T
32002

Class I3 4-4-2T
32078   32079   32084   32091

Class K 2-6-0
32350   32351   32352   32353

Class C2 0-6-0
32441   32451   32527   32532   32552
32445   32522   32529   32545   32553

Class E4 0-6-2T
32465   32484   32497   32519
32480   32496   32516   32520

Class E5 0-6-2T
32571   32584

Total 31

Allocations: 1959

Class H 0-4-4T
31162   31269   31530

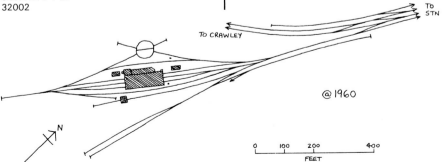

TO STN

TO CRAWLEY

@ 1960

N

0   100   200   400
FEET

Class K 2-6-0
| 32344 | 32346 | 32348 | 32351 | 32353 |
| 32345 | 32347 | 32350 | 32352 | |

Class C2 0-6-0
| 32523 | 32528 | 32532 | 32535 |
| 32527 | 32529 | 32534 | 32536 |

Class 4 2-6-4T
| 42068 | 42069 | 42070 | 42071 |

Class 4 4-6-0
75075

Class 4 2-6-4T
| 80010 | 80011 | 80012 |

Total 28

Three Bridges shed closed in January 1964 and its remaining locos went to Guildford 70C, Bournemouth 70F, Brighton 75A and Feltham 70B. The shed continued to store and service visiting engines up to November of the same year.

The south-western end of Three Bridges shed in 1958 with three of its Class C2 0-6-0 allocation facing. Left to right are Nos 32534, 32536 and 32523. W. Potter

The north-eastern entrance to Three Bridges in 1963. Nearest the camera is Class Q1 0-6-0 No 33015 (75E). K. Fairey

Class C2 0-6-0 No 32535 (75E) being coaled at Three Bridges in 1961. R. C. Riley

Two BR Standard designs at Three Bridges in 1963. K. Fairey

75F TUNBRIDGE WELLS WEST

Pre-Grouping Origin: LBSCR
Gazetteer Ref: 5 D5
Closed: 1965
Shed-Code: 75F (1950 to 1963)
Allocations: 1950

Class H 0-4-4T

31016	31182

Class I3 4-4-2T

32021	32026	32029	32087
32022	32027	32075	32090
32023	32028	32082	

Class J1 4-6-2T

32325

Class J2 4-6-2T
32326

Class D3 0-4-4T
32390

Class E4 0-6-2T
32512   32582

Class 4MT 2-6-4T
42096   42098   42100
42097   42099   42101

Total 24

Allocations: 1959

Class H 0-4-4T
31278   31327   31521   31554
31310   31329   31544

Class E4 0-6-2T
32517   32581

Class 2 2-6-2T
41319

Class 4 2-6-4T
42101   42103   42105
42102   42104   42106

Class 4 2-6-4T
80014   80016   80018
80015   80017   80019

Total 22

Tunbridge Wells West lost its independent status in September 1963 when it became a sub-shed to Brighton 75A. The locos transferred to Brighton 75A and Three Bridges 75E.

It later became a sub-shed to Redhill 75B with the closure of Brighton in June 1964. The depot continued under Redhill's wing until final closure in June 1965.

An overall view of the shed yard and station approach at Tunbridge Wells West in 1951. On the left Class I3 4-4-2T No 32023 (75F) is taking on water. This class of loco formed the mainstay of the shed's tank classes in 1950, but all had been withdrawn or transferred away by late 1951.
R. C. Riley

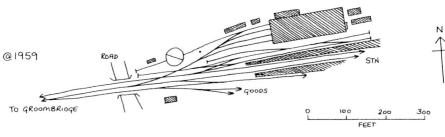

94

Tunbridge Wells West shed in 1954 clearly showing the scant remains of the original roof which was rebuilt soon after. B. Hilton

Tunbridge Wells West in the month it became a sub-shed to Brighton 75A, September 1963. W. T. Stubbs

This 1958 view of Tunbridge Wells West depicts the new roof and two of the depot's Class H 0-4-4T locos Nos 31554 (left) and 31521. K. Fairey

75G EASTBOURNE

Pre-Grouping Origin: LBSCR
Gazetteer Ref: 5 G5
Closed: 1965
Shed-Codes: 75G (1950 to 1952)
Allocations: 1950

Class I1X 4-4-2T
32009   32603

Class I3 4-4-2T
32030   32077   32081   32083   32089

Class B4 4-4-0
32043   32055   32062   32068   32072
32054   32060   32063   32071   32073

Class K 2-6-0
32348

Class D3 0-4-4T
32385   32394

Class E5 0-6-2T
32402   32405   32574   32591
32404   32406   32588   32593

Class C2 0-6-0
32434   32534   32538

Class E4 0-6-2T
32485   32518

Total 33

Eastbourne shed lost its code and engine allocation in September 1952. The majority of the locos went to Brighton 75A, Tunbridge Wells West 75F, Redhill 75B and St Leonards 74E.

It then became sub-shed to Brighton 75A and was allowed to depreciate structurally, becoming virtually roofless by 1956.

When Brighton closed in June 1964, Redhill 75B became the parent depot until final closure in June 1965.

The southern end of Eastbourne shed in 1950

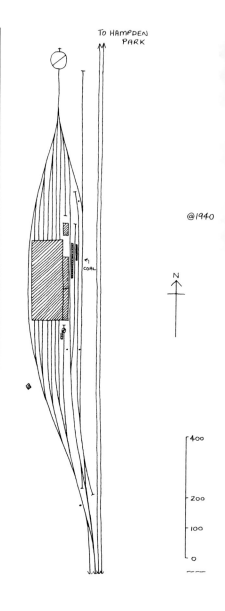

TO HAMPDEN PARK

@1940

N

400
200
100
0

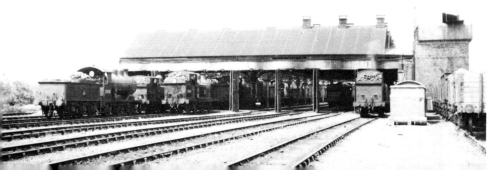

Looking south inside the roofless Eastbourne in 1960 whilst operating as a sub-shed of Brighton 75A.   T. Wright

Class E4 0-6-2T No 2562 (eventual BR No 32562) being coaled at Eastbourne in 1933.   H. C. Casserley

The more decrepit north entrance to Eastbourne in the same year, 1950. B. Hilton

List of Shed-Codes

The following list sets out every shed-code that existed for steam Motive Power Depots under the Southern Region from 1950 to 1967 along with each venue and its length of occupancy.

70A Nine Elms 1950-67
70B Feltham 1950-67
70C Guildford 1950-67
70D Basingstoke 1950-63. Eastleigh 1963-67
70E Reading South 1950-59. Salisbury 1962-67
70F Fratton 1954-59. Bournemouth 1963-67
70G Newport IoW 1954-57. Weymouth 1963-67
70H Ryde IoW 1954-67
70I Southampton Docks 1963-66

71A Eastleigh 1950-63
71B Bournemouth 1950-63
71C Dorchester 1950-55
71D Fratton 1950-54
71E Newport IoW 1950-54.
71F Ryde IoW 1950-54
71G Bath Green Park 1950-58. Weymouth 1958-63
71H Templecombe 1950-58. Yeovil Pen Mill 1958-59
71I Southampton Docks 1950-63
71J Highbridge 1950-58

72A Exmouth Junction 1950-63
72B Salisbury 1950-62
72C Yeovil Town 1950-63
72D Plymouth Friary 1950-58
72E Barnstaple Junction 1950-63
72F Wadebridge 1950-63

73A Stewarts Lane 1950-62
73B Bricklayers Arms 1950-62
73C Hither Green 1950-61
73D Gillingham 1950-59
73E Faversham 1950-59
73F Ashford 1958-63
73G Ramsgate 1958-59
73H Dover 1958-61
73J Tonbridge 1958-62

74A Ashford 1950-58
74B Ramsgate 1950-58
74C Dover 1950-58
74D Tonbridge 1950-58
74E St Leonards 1950-58

75A Brighton 1950-64
75B Redhill 1950-65
75C Norwood Junction 1950-64
75D Horsham 1950-59. Stewarts Lane 1962-63
75E Three Bridges 1950-64
75F Tunbridge Wells West 1950-63
75G Eastbourne 1950-52

Guildford on the last day of steam on the Southern Region — 9 July 1967. BR Standard Class 5MT 4-6-0 No 73155 takes on water overlooked by the shed pilot No 30072. T. Wright

Roundhouse depots had a distinct advantage for ease of shunting movements except when the turntable required attention and trapped all within as is the case here at Guildford in June 1963. K. Fairey

A spotless 'Battle of Britain' 4-6-2, No 34064
Fighter Command, *outside Eastleigh shed in May*
1964.   K. Fairey

Bournemouth shed a few days before closure in July 1959 with an unidentified 4-6-2 amid its successors. J. L. Stevenson

The approach to Bath Green Park's ex-SDJR building in 1959. Photomatic

Southampton Docks depot in February 1960 with four camera-shy 'USA' 0-6-0Ts Nos 30070, 30067, 30074 and 30071.   T. Wright

The single lane sub-shed at Exmouth as seen from the station platform in July 1957. Left to right are Nos 41307, 30670, 41318 and 41306 (all 72A). N. E. Preedy

A familiar sight during the latter days of steam —
Salisbury shed in August 1966.   J. L. Stevenson

Salisbury in happier times with BR Standard and
ex-GWR locos sharing the metals. 'Hall' class 4-6-0
No 6932 Burwarton Hall (86C) is on the right:
Photomatic

Yeovil Town shed just before nationalisation with
Class T9 4-4-0 No 114 (BR No 30114).
LGRP courtesy of David & Charles

The coaling and watering facilities at Plymouth Friary
as viewed from the West in 1958.   K. Fairey

Southern Railway Class T1 0-4-4T No 7 (BR
No 30007) outside the eastern end of Plymouth
Friary shed in 1949. The last few survivors of this
class were withdrawn in 1951.   B. K. B. Green

Contrasting views of the same depot — Gillingham.
The livelier of the two depicts the shed in 1951 with
a variety of motive power including a WD class
2-8-0 No 90226. The other was taken in 1963,
three years after closure.
Photomatic & W. T. Stubbs

A view of Ashford shed in Southern days.
Photomatic

*Redhill shed in 1935 showing the style of roof prior
to the 1950 rebuilt by BR.*
LGRP courtesy of David & Charles

A pre-grouping study of the LBSCR depot at Three Bridges in 1921. LGRP courtesy of David & Charles

Index